BE KIND AND
TAKE NO SH★T

BE KIND AND TAKE NO SH★T

A Woman's Guide to Balance, Power & Joy

Heather Gwaltney

ISBN: 978-1-7339396-0-7

Sure Shot

"...I Want To Say a Little Something
That's Long Overdue

The Disrespect To Women Has Got To Be Through

To All The Mothers And Sisters
And The Wives And Friends

I Want To Offer My Love And Respect To The End..."
- Beastie Boys

Dedication

To women everywhere.

Contents

Introduction

We know it's tough being a woman. We are often told to keep our sensitivity in check — to smile and play nice. We are raised to follow a path of safety in a world that claims to be logical, controlled and linear. Often to get ahead, we also think we have to act like men.

My intention with this book is to hold women up by sharing the knowledge I've gained through my education and over 20 years of experience in the private, non-profit and spiritual worlds.

In it, I talk about honoring our sensitivity, how to meditate in a very easy way, the transformative nature and misconceptions of forgiveness, and much more. There's even a chapter on dating!

In each chapter, I take spiritual concepts and apply them to real-life experiences that are both grounded in reality and reflect the often absurd, humorousness of life. Then I back up the stories with scientific data, and close each chapter with an activity, that guides you, step by step, on how to apply the concepts to your own life.

By the end you will:

- Be reminded of your worthiness;
- Have more tools to cope with life's crazy, to be more authentic, happy and empowered; and
- Be better able to offer the world the best you have.

As women, I believe it's our responsibility to stand by each other. What the world needs now is the power of women working together, in our authenticity and at our full potential.

Enjoy and keep in touch!

Meme graphic by iMeme.

Chapter 1

Highly Sensitive People.
Are you one of them?

Growing up, I was able to read people and feel their happiness and pain as if they were my own. Often, it was hard being able to tell whether the feelings were mine or theirs. Sometimes, witnessing people's pain felt unbearable. I always imagined I was one of those babies who reacted to the slightest environmental change – like a pin dropping or a light switch being turned on or off. At times, I felt like I was a person looking at a situation from the outside, so different from the people around me. I wasn't relating to them, yet could feel almost everything.

At an early adult age, I was steamrolled by men who wanted to have sex with and/or date me; and sometimes I'd go along with it primarily because I couldn't tell what feelings where theirs vs. mine. Over many years, I've learned to be cautious about who I let into my intimate space, both friends and romantic partners. Only after years of meditation (and now Reiki), I am also able to see the difference between my feelings and others most of the time.

Now, I will look at a person and get an immediate feeling about whether they are generally good or bad. I'm repelled by people with dark or dodgy energy. I love connecting with people, yet also need time alone to regain my energy. Dramatic situations stress me out (aside from a good show on Netflix!), yet I appreciate emotional intimacy.

Recently, I learned about the term HSP or Highly Sensitive Person, and it all made sense. Finally, I understood why I have a tendency to:

- Have an extreme sensitivity to physical sensations; I can feel it all deeply!
- Get overwhelmed by external stimulation
- Deeply process and reflect on information I'm exposed to
- Be deeply moved by music, movies and even trees!

It's deep!

Photo by Mick Schultz, MixPix

THE SCIENCE BEHIND IT

The term and concept of a Highly Sensitive Person (HSP) officially exists; it's a thing. Publicly conceptualized in 1997 by Aron & Aron, HSPs are individuals who have a high Sensory Processing Sensitivity (SPS), an overactive nervous system, if you will, and it's something we're born with.

I first learned about HSP research through articles in *Psychology Today and Forbes* (interestingly enough). Often linked to being introverted, Dr. Marwa Azab explains in her *Psychology Today* article[1] that only "30% of HSPs are thought to be extroverts." But let's remember; introverts and extroverts can both be very social. The difference lies in where the person gets their energy, either through being quiet and having alone time or through being around others.

In the *Forbes* article, "9 Signs You're A Highly Sensitive Person[2]," author Travis Bradberry cited psychologist, Dr. Elaine Aron and her work of "using MRI scans of highly sensitive people's brains..." The scans revealed "that they experience sounds, feelings, and even the presence of other people much more intensely than the average person." Here, I also learned that "...genes are responsible for the 15-20% of people who qualify as 'highly sensitive.'"

Dr. Elaine Aron, who is the pioneer in HSP research and literature, has coined an acronym that encapsulates the

1 Azab, M. Ph.D., (2017, July). Are You a Highly Sensitive Person? Should You Change? A sensitive person's brain is different: Research points to some advantages by. *Psychology Today.*
2 Bradberry, T. (2016, August). 9 Signs You're A Highly Sensitive Person. *Forbes.*

unique traits of an HSP. The acronym is DOES and is broken down as follows:

Depth of processing information with a pattern of observing and reflecting before we act,

Overstimulation caused by a tendency to pay more attention to and be more affected by things, which can lead to being overwhelmed,

Emphasis given to emotional reactions with our strong sense of empathy, and

Sensing subtleties.

But don't just take Dr. Aron's word for it! In just one of her summaries[3], she cites an additional 14 studies related to HSP characteristics. Included among them are studies on the genetic variation in HSPs that cause lower serotonin. Additionally, research indicates that HSPs experience more activity in the brain's insula and mirror neuron systems. According to Michael Pluess and Ilona Boniwell in their study of adolescent girls struggling with depression[4], those who scored high on SPS (being synonymous with HSP) responded more favorably to positive interventions than those who scored low on SPS. In other words, those who participated in the study with high SPS scores scored lower on depression after the intervention than their low SPS counterparts.

The good news is that an HSP can more easily identify and respond to feelings, both their own and others. They

---

3 Aron, E. (1997). *The Highly Sensitive Person.*
4 Boniwell, M. and Boniwell, P. (2015, August). *Sensory-Processing Sensitivity predicts treatment response to a school-based depression prevention program: Evidence of Vantage Sensitivity.*

can also listen and read people more accurately through body language, tone of voice and other subtleties. The challenge for an HSP is to manage those intense feelings. As Bradberry says, "only after understanding that they are highly sensitive can the HSP benefit from their heightened emotional awareness."

Pros and cons of being an HSP
In summary, the pros of being an HSP, according to research include:

- The ability to adapt to diverse environments
- Increased ability to learn new material and learn from mistakes
- Better decision-making skills
- The ability to gain greater mental health from positive life experiences
- Ability to sense danger and opportunities that others miss
- Tendency to be highly conscientious and intuitive.

Even though I list some of the cons of being an HSP second, they will likely strike you at first, since they can make your life more difficult. If you are an HSP, you are also more likely to be:

- At higher risk for depression
- At higher risk for anxiety
- More deeply affected by environmental stressors leading to overstimulation
- Often inhibited and/or fearful
- Overwhelmed by the feeling of being different and/or flawed
- More averse to criticism, negativity and stress.

Photo by Mick Schultz, MixPix

NEXT STEP – ARE YOU AN HSP?

How about you?

1. Do you feel other people's feelings as if they were your own?
2. Are you sometimes drained by stimulating environments and/or people who talk too much?
3. Are you turned off from and drained by mainstream TV news?
4. Do you have a visceral reaction to loud noises?

If you answered yes to any one or more of these questions, you may be an HSP. Take a test to see if you are, and access resources on Dr. Elaine Aron's website at hsperson.com.

About HSP and what follows

I've opened this book with a chapter on HSPs because it is the lens through which I see and feel the world. Being a personality type only explored and studied in the last 20 years, I also wanted to identify these set of characteristics as legitimate, so those who are an HSP will know that there are others who have similar levels of sensitivity and that they are not crazy. And for those who know HSPs, you may gain a greater insight into their reactions towards you.

In the upcoming chapters, I share my thoughts on a number of topics that I think women need to know more about, whether they are an HSP or not. The topics I cover are relevant to women in general, yet in each chapter I will include a brief description of how the topic may affect HSPs specifically.

Disclaimer

The information in this book is intended for your educational use only and is not a substitute for professional medical advice, diagnosis or treatment. Always seek the advice of your physician or other qualified health provider(s) if you have questions regarding a medical condition.

That I Would Be Good

That I would be good even if I did nothing
That I would be good even if I got the thumbs down
That I would be good if I got and stayed sick
That I would be good even if I gained ten pounds
That I would be fine even if I went bankrupt
That I would be good if I lost my hair and my youth
That I would be great if I was no longer queen
That I would be grand if I was not all knowing
That I would be loved even when I numb myself
That I would be good even when I am overwhelmed
That I would be loved even when I was fuming
That I would be good even if I was clingy
That I would be good even if I lost sanity
That I would be good...

— Alanis Morissette

#honoryourfeelings

"You are living, you occupy space, you have mass.

You Matter."

-Albert Einstein

Chapter 2

Energy exists,
so don't look at me like that!

Energy is a funny thing; unless you are part of a spiritual community, people really don't acknowledge or talk about it. I've been doing energy work for nearly 20 years now – yet, when I tell people about it, many will nod and smile silently as if what I'm saying is some kind of hippy dippy crap that has no basis in reality. I was raised in Northern California, but I also remember being taught about energy as a child, in my science classes! It exists according to Western belief systems, right? So why do people react this way?

In the early 2000's, a girlfriend of mine stumbled across an organization called BPI (Berkeley Psychic Institute). Yes, this kind of place exists – it was in Berkeley, CA after all! In any case, the friend encouraged me to check out a workshop with her on energy. At the time, I thought, *wow, that sounds pretty weird. Sure, why not?* Two years later, I had taken a full set of energy curriculum from BPI about how to protect myself energetically, how to read and heal others energetically and how to bring more of what I wanted into my life with visualizations. Although it's important to protect ourselves and bring in more of what we want into our lives, I thought a higher level of spirituality was to learn how to be intimate with others in a safe way and grow collectively. In the end, life is about interdependence and unity, right? So, I left BPI and integrated the good that I learned there into my existing meditation practice.

Fast forward 15 years or so, I dated someone who was a Reiki Master, another foreign concept! I was intrigued and had been interested in learning more for a while. So, I met his Reiki teacher and ended up taking a number of classes through her, including Reiki One, Two and Three (Master Level). I'm now a Reiki Master.

A note about Reiki: You may be wondering, "What is this woman involved with now? And what in the heck is Reiki?" I can't speak to the former, but I can provide a definition of Reiki. Simply described, Reiki is another form of healing where the Reiki practitioner uses their hands (either by light touch or by holding them two to three inches away from the body of the recipient) to channel energy to themselves (in the case of self-Reiki) or to the recipient, activating the recipient's natural healing processes of the body. This is all done to restore physical and emotional balance, and well-being.

As an HSP

As an HSP (remember that's Highly Sensitive Person), I am particularly sensitive to energy ups and downs, mostly, the downs that come from negative, over-sensationalized media, negative people and the overstimulation that is typical in American life. That is what drew me to do energy work in the first place, in addition to the meditation (read more in Chapter: *Meditation. Do it.*). But don't be fooled! Even non-HSPs are affected by energy.

THE SCIENCE BEHIND IT

The concept of energy was developed by Aristotle, and "energy" as a word, has been most commonly translated in the English dictionary as "being at work." Energy was first used in the English language in the 17th century as power.

In the 19th century, Julius Robert von Mayer, James Prescott Joule and Hermann Ludwig Ferdinand von Helmholtz used the term "living force" to refer to energy when they formulated what is known today as the 1st Law of Thermodynamics, which postulates that energy cannot be created or destroyed.

In the 20th century, Albert Einstein linked concepts of energy and mass in his Theory of Relativity.

Let's talk more about the science of energy based on what most of us learned in elementary school. Everything in the universe is made up of matter and energy. In physics, energy is a property of matter. Matter can be transferred between objects and converted in form. Matter describes the physical things around us: the earth, the air we breathe and physical inanimate objects, such as a computer or piece of furniture. It's anything that has mass and occupies space. Matter is made up of atoms and atoms consist of a nucleus surrounded by electrons. The atom is mostly comprised of space, however, and in this space, we hold energetic vibrations at the cellular level. A graphic of an atom illustrates this below.

Atom structure

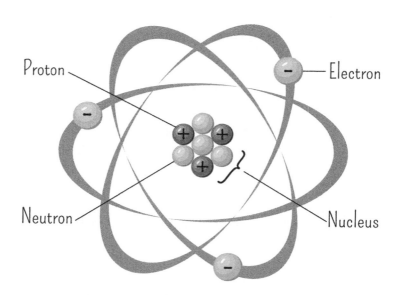

Eastern religion and philosophy both address energy by differentiating between the physical and non-physical bodies. According to many Indian traditions, humans exist in two parallel dimensions – the physical body and the subtle body (which represents psychology, emotions and the mind). "Chakras are also referred to as subtle body and spirit body – in both Eastern and Western cultures", according to Geoffrey Samuel and Jay Johnston[5], both professors of religious studies known for their research on yoga and esoteric traditions. "There are seven 'main' chakras, although some say there are as many as 114." Furthermore, the health of the subtle body or chakras is directly connected to the health of the physical body.

---

5 Geoffrey Samuel and Jay Johnston (August 4, 2015). *Religion and the Subtle Body in Asia and the West: Between Mind and Body.*

These subtle body chakras are thought of as spinning disks or wheels, representing energy focal points in the body. According to Buddhist and Hindu traditions, the seven chakras are aligned in a column along the spinal cord, starting at its base (the 1st Chakra) moving to the top of the head (the 7th Chakra). The chakras also correspond to specific physiological traits, such as the need for survival in the first chakra, a person's power center in their third chakra and a person's ability to give and receive love in the fourth chakra. Although people perceive and practice chakra work differently, the most common model, which I follow, is shown in both the graphic and table below.

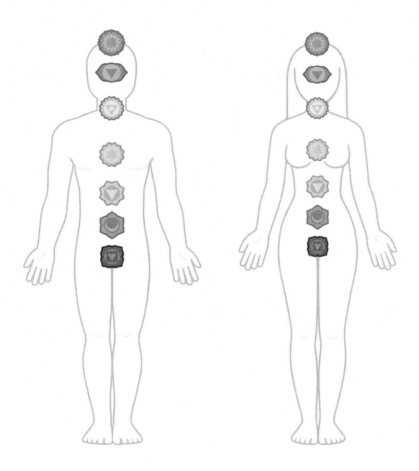

Chakra	Body	Color	Association
First chakra	Base of the spine/sacrum	Red	Survival, money, security
Second chakra	Lower belly/genital region	Orange	Sex and creativity
Third chakra	Stomach/solar plexus	Yellow	Power center, control
Fourth chakra	Heart	Green/Pink	Affinity and ability to love and connect
Fifth chakra	Throat	Light Blue	Power of your voice, Speaking your truth
Sixth chakra	3rd eye	Indigo/Dark Blue	Allows you to see beyond 5 senses Manifest through vision
Seventh chakra	Top of the head/crown	Purple	Connects you to universal intelligence

If we are to compare this back to Western science, we can define the subtle body as energy within the atom, while the physical body is represented by matter. And, as with Western science where energy is part of matter, matter and energy in the Eastern tradition are also interconnected as the physical and subtle bodies. In both histories and traditions, there is a clear connection between mind/body – matter/energy – physical/subtle chakra body. They are equally valid mental constructs; just defined differently.

Next Step - Working With Light
We've covered a lot with a description of energy. Let's look more closely at the colors associated with each chakra or spinning energy "wheel" in the body (refer to diagram and table above). Many visualize these colors as light. Colors of light I work with often are purple, gold/yellow and light blue/baby blue. As a reminder, purple light is associated with our 7th chakra – the energy center that connects us to the Universe/Spirit/G-force. Purple is a very high-vibration color and is used as a form of healing and transformation. It also happens to be one of my favorite colors!

In the morning, I imagine that my body is completely surrounded by purple light with a gold rim. When I'm feeling down or am in a negative thought loop, I refocus my attention on purple or golden yellow light, imagining it filling up my space, while also focusing on my breath. Practicing this helps me shift my energy and strengthen my ability to focus (refer to Chapter: Meditation. Do it.).

Photo by Mick Schultz, MixPix

To work with energy yourself, you can easily replicate what I do, but pick any color that you are drawn to in the moment – it doesn't have to be purple! There are a number of other colors to choose from with different associations (again, refer to chakra section above). The most important thing for you though is how you associate with that color. Pick one that you like, even if it's what you happen to like just in that moment. Maybe you're attracted to red light or need the healing feeling of green light.

If you're in a black mood, however, imagining black, brown, or even gray is associated with blocked energy and not recommended. Many spiritualists will recommend focusing on white light. I, however, have been taught that white light is associated with death. You've heard the jovial phrase "step away from the (white) light." Yellow/gold is as light as I go, but pick something that works for you!

Just a Ride

Life, it's ever so strange
It's so full of change
Think that you've worked it out
Then BANG
Right out of the blue
Something happens to you
To throw you off course
And then you
Breakdown
Yeah you breakdown
Well don't you breakdown
Listen to me
Because
It's just a ride, it's just a ride
No need to run, no need to hide
It'll take you round and round
Sometimes you're up
Sometimes you're down
It's just a ride, it's just a ride
Don't be scared
Don't hide your eyes
It may feel so real inside
But don't forget it's just a ride
Truth, we don't want to hear
It's too much to take
Don't like to feel out of control
So we make our plans
Ten times a day
And when they don't go
Our way we

Breakdown
Yeah we breakdown
Well don't you breakdown
Listen to me
Because
It's just a ride, it's just a ride
No need to run, no need to hide
It'll take you round and round
Sometimes you're up
Sometimes you're down
It's just a ride, it's just a ride
Don't be scared
Don't hide your eyes
It may feel so real inside
But don't forget it's just a ride...

-Jem

#energyunitesus

Photo of Tina Fey from Saturday Night Live, NBC.com.

Chapter 3

Your beliefs are your reality. Really, they are.

"Scary Monsters" X-files Season 9, Episode 14

A young boy believes in monsters and has watched them kill his mother. Now, anyone who comes near the boy is killed. After seeing this happen firsthand, the boy's father is also now afraid of the monsters and any danger they may bring to people around him. In an effort to solve this X-File, John Doggett and his partner, Monica Reyes, visit the boy and his father in a remote location in the woods. As the boy draws his visions of the monsters, they come to life, threatening the lives of both John and Monica. John begins being attacked by them, but then realizes, as the typical non-believer of the duo, that he does not believe in the boy's visions. Within seconds, as if by a miracle, the monsters disappear and he is no longer in danger. John then goes on to save his partner by way of convincing her that the monsters are simply the boy's imagination or belief. She too is then freed from the monsters. And the story's message is revealed–your beliefs become your reality.

This, of course, is science fiction, but you can see that it creatively, yet astutely, depicts the powers of the mind and illustrates how powerful a belief can be.

Like the "Scary Monsters" episode, most of us can relate to having "monsters" in our head. As an HSP who processes information deeply, I tend to have repetitive thought patterns and cycles, which can get caught in a negative loop. The challenge with this type of fixation is obvious, but there is also a positive side to it that may surprise you. For instance, if I'm conscious enough of my thinking in the moment, I will catch the thought pattern in action and simply (with mindful focus) switch my attention to a positive thought or image and then become fixated on that new positive thought or imagery. Having a tendency to become fixated usually translates to attachment. Although general attachment to objects is looked down upon by meditators; in this case, it can serve us. You see, if you just shift the object of your obsession/attachment, you can then become attached to something positive, which translates after practice and repetition to a new thought pattern and/or behavior. It personally helps me to stick with and commit to new behaviors. Need a new mantra? "Get fixated on the good stuff."

THE SCIENCE BEHIND IT

In a recent article, "The Metaphysics of Defeating Trump: It starts with the power of a thought[6]," author Mitch Horowitz provides examples of what a person can achieve by having a "single-minded goal" that is also "specific, concrete, and...achievable, even if greatly bold." Although the article is largely focused on current President Donald Trump, as the title implies, he compares and contrasts two political figures and the success

---

6 Horowitz, M. (2018, September). The Metaphysics of Defeating Trump: It starts with the power of a thought by. *Medium*.

that followed the power of their positive thoughts. He first describes how, Trump, as someone who exhibits a "showman's powers of persuasion and self-invention", can prove to be "grotesquely effective." Although, Trump has "structured a life around the unethical attainment of power," the truthful observer can agree that, even though he may not have a realistic view of his own capabilities, the mere focus on goals and achieving them has helped him reach those goals.

In the other example, Horowitz shifts his attention to Cory Booker, current New Jersey Senator, who in 1996 was even thought "to become President one day" by his peers. After being a "Rhodes scholar and student at Yale Law School...Cory quickly rose to become the nationally prominent mayor of Newark, New Jersey, and then a senator and prospective running mate for candidate Hillary Clinton." Sure these are anecdotal examples, but they are still very powerful.

Now let's take a look at what happens physiologically with thoughts and belief systems. In her article, "How Your Thoughts Change Your Brain, Cells and Genes[7]," Debbie Hampton defines a thought as "...an electrochemical event taking place in your nerve cells producing a cascade of physiological changes."

Science tells us that "thoughts cause the brain to release neurotransmitters, which are chemical messengers that communicate within the brain and to the nervous system." Neurotransmitters are incredibly powerful because they "control almost all of your body's functions,

---

7 Hampton, D. (2018, January). How Your Thoughts Change Your Brain, Cells and Genes. *The Best Brain Possible.*

from hormones to digestion, to the feeling of joy, regret or anxiety."

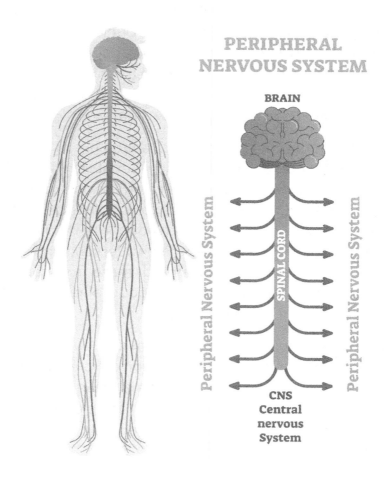

So, our thoughts are affecting the neurotransmitters which then attach themselves to the thousands of receptors that are attached to each cell in body. To further complicate, yet illuminate the situation, "when we have feelings of anger, anxiety, excitement or happiness, each separate emotion releases its own peptides, changing the overall structure of each cell. If a cell has been exposed to a certain peptide more than others, the new cell that is produced will have more of the receptor that matches with that specific peptide," says Hampton.

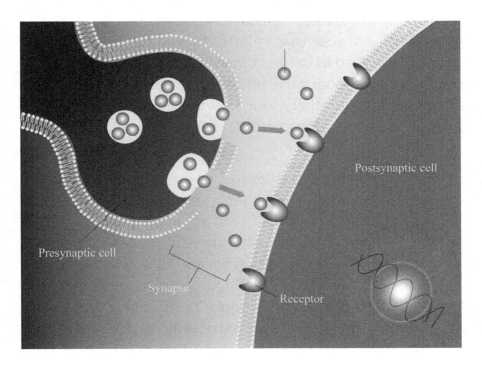

Put more simply, the more negative peptides or negative thoughts you have, the more receptive your cells are to the same types of negative peptides in the future, also thereby reducing the positive peptide receptors.

Shifting our thoughts can shift our biology

Although this biological function is interesting, it can also be alarming if we become too attached and defeatist about our past experiences, thoughts and emotions.

Let's be clear though; our biological and psychological history does not determine our destiny. By shifting our thoughts and perceptions, we are able to literally control our biology.

Indian (Hindu and Buddhist) religions and philosophies would refer to this as *samskaras*. I liken this to a mental and emotional scar that is left when we've had a painful experience. And in order to heal the scar, we must allow ourselves to process the emotion(s) associated with the experience. Essentially, our power lies in the way we 1) process our emotions and 2) perceive and respond to situations.

Licensed Physician and Integrative Medicine Advocate, Deepak Chopra, "argues that everything that happens in the mind and brain is physically represented elsewhere in the body, with mental states (thoughts, feelings, perceptions and memories) directly influencing physiology by means of neurotransmitters..." He believes that we as individuals (with our mind, body and consciousness) are "inextricably woven into" our external worlds (our relationships and environment) as part of "a single process." Therefore, "by influencing one, (we) influence everything."[8]

Refocusing our thoughts to positivity
Teacher and Clinical Psychologist, Talya Steinberg, Psy.D. states that "resilient people actually resist illnesses, cope with adversity, and recover more quickly because they are able to maintain positive thinking and

---

8 Chopra, D. (n.d.). approach to healthcare section. Retrieved from Wikipedia.

manage their stress effectively." She goes on to say that "by managing our attitudes and stress levels, we actually control neurochemical transmissions in the body."[9]

Yet even more positive is what Dr. Breuning, Professor Emerita at California State University, has to say about how to actually build new neural pathways. She claims that this is possible by practicing positive thinking consistently over a six-week period by giving "the electricity in your brain an alternative place to flow." For instance, when you get caught up in a negative thought or reaction to a situation, simply shift your mind to a more positive thought, perspective and/or response.

An HSP?

If you think you're too overwhelmed and too sensitive to reprogram your thoughts, think again! There has been at least one study on young women and depression with the outcome that once exposed to positive interventions, they were able to elevate their mood more so than non-HSPs (refer to Chapter 1: Highly Sensitive People. Are you one of them?). You may just struggle with the confidence to believe that this is the case. Try my exercise below to see what's possible.

NEXT STEP – INVENTORY YOUR BELIEFS

While studying Reiki, my teacher would habitually tell me to write down my belief systems about any given topic that I felt blocked or burdened by. Begrudgingly, I would journal about them out of pure will, and by doing

9 Breazeale, R. Ph.D. and Steinberg, T, Psy.D, (2012, July). Thoughts, Neurotransmitters, Body-Mind Connection. *Psychology Today.*

so, I would often gain clarity about the said belief system that would ultimately lead to becoming unstuck.

Photo by Mick Schultz, MixPix.

Now it's your turn! To shed light on any given part of your life that is not working for you, write down your belief(s) about that topic. If you want a more comprehensive purge, make an inventory of your beliefs to see whether or not they are true and if they are serving you.

Often what happens when you transparently look at your beliefs in a curious, non-judgmental way, you see that 1) they are often misguided and not rooted in reality 2) they are creating your reality and 3) they can even be absurd and humorous.

If you're truly feeling ambitious, add a list of those things that you're passionate about. Ask yourself, "What matters to me?" and "What do I care about?" Write all about it!

When you give voice to what's in your head and heart, it's a powerful step in letting go and creating new belief systems that will shape your life in miraculous ways!

Finally Woken

Finally woken, finally woken
I've been thinking 'bout things
For a long while
I'm feeling so calm
I've got a big smile
I have a view of the sun
Right over the sea
And now I can feel
Life is flowing through me
You see I've finally woken
From a long sleep
I'm ready to jump
To make that blind leap
Coz I now believe
I have the power in me
I've got the faith baby
I can truly be free
Finally woken
Finally woken
Child don't worry it's okay
The sun is out for another day
And I say it'll be alright
Today's the first day of the
Rest of your life
Remember, remember,
Remember this, remember
Child don't worry it's okay
The sun is out for another day
And I say it'll be alright
Today's the first day of the

Rest of your life
Remember remember
Remember this remember
Child don't worry it's okay
The sun is out for another day
Today's the first day of the
Rest of your life...
And I say it'll be alright, be alright

–Jem

#watchwhatsinyourhead

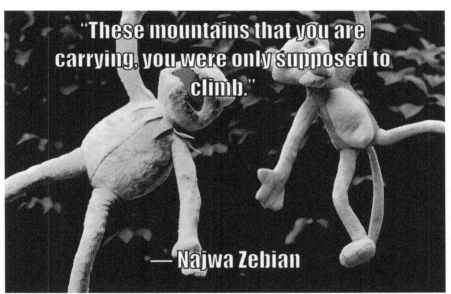

"These mountains that you are carrying, you were only supposed to climb."

— Najwa Zebian

Meme graphic by iMeme.

Chapter 4

Forgiveness is about letting go, and it will transform you.

Forgiveness is often a misunderstood practice; that's why people tend to struggle so much with it and consequently, why they hold onto pain (which ultimately only hurts the person carrying it).

Myths about forgiveness
- Forgiveness is about telling someone what they did was okay.
- In order to forgive, we have to lower our standards.
- If we forgive someone, we give him/her permission to do what they did again.
- If we forgive someone, we are also supposed to forget what she/he did.
- The other person must ask for forgiveness before it can be given.
- The other person must still be in our lives or at the very least, still be alive in order to be forgiven.

Facts about forgiveness
- Forgiveness is about letting go of the pain we hold onto in response to someone else's behavior.
- Forgiveness is personal; it's more about how we are responding to a painful situation, as opposed

to specifically what another person has done to us.

- We do not need to forget what the person has done in order to forgive them.
- Forgiving someone is not telling him/her that what she/he did was okay; it's merely releasing the pain we have in response to what they've done.
- The other person does not need to ask for forgiveness before you forgive them. In fact, we can even forgive someone who is deceased.
- We can even forgive ourselves, and it's actually the perfect place to start.
- Forgiving someone frees us and opens us up to feel deeply and receive more of what we want in our lives.
- We must first allow ourselves to feel the pain associated with the experience in order to let it go and forgive. The result is healing.

You've heard the phrase, 'just let it go,' right? We hear this particularly when someone has just pissed us off, but hearing this in the moment may piss us off even more! In any case, there's a reason why this phrase has become a cliché.

Some of us, especially HSPs, absorb the feelings of others like a sponge – and we can be consumed by them, perhaps in order to heal the situation and/or because we've had a similar experience in the past. We may continue to relive the experience until we address the underlying feelings in order to let them go. But how can we let them go?

Moving Your Energy

Moving your energy is a great place to start! It can definitely get you unstuck, and there are a number of ways to move and release energy, feelings and experiences. My personal favorites are through laughing, exercise and sex/orgasm. Meditation and Reiki are also powerful. The body's most basic ways of doing this are through yawning, crying, burping and my least favorite (yet necessary) …farting. You can see there are so many options to choose from!

Every morning, I meditate or do self-Reiki. I refer to this as a non-negotiable practice as it gets me grounded and refreshed for the day. If I've had a particularly stressful day or have been exposed to more than usual amounts of toxicity, I will either meditate again, go to the gym or go for a run. I also use humor throughout the day to cope with life's daily absurdities.

But all of that is general upkeep.

What if you feel overwhelmed by darkness or experience something specifically troublesome? I've got an example for that! Just last week, I was driving to work and a rather strong, shameful feeling came over me. At first, it wasn't clear what experience the feeling reflected, so I simply allowed it to be there. Trying to remember when I felt that same type of feeling, I was reminded of a relationship I'd had four years prior that was very emotionally difficult and at times, degrading. I felt so upset that I'd allowed myself to be degraded (both then and now). Again, I allowed all of the feelings to be there and gently wept as I continued to drive. Minutes later, I felt a release and was brought back to a sense of neutrality and balance.

THE SCIENCE BEHIND IT

First of all, who knew there was a science behind forgiveness? The common theme across the research is compassion and empathy, usually directed towards ourselves initially and then towards the person we have felt wronged by. What's most compelling about the research, however, is it's all about us (the receiver) of the hurtful experience and not the one who has wronged us.

Although some people are considered to be more forgiving types, the best news about forgiveness is that we can become better at it through practice. Clinical Psychologist Dr. Rubin Khoddam defines forgiveness as the choice "to accept what happened as it happened rather than what could or should have happened." He lists the three common components that define forgiveness (as represented by various research):

1. "Gaining a more balanced view of the offender and the event;
2. Decreasing negative feelings towards the offender and potentially increasing compassion; and
3. Giving up the right to punish the offender or to demand restitution."

Dr. Khoddam continues by saying that forgiveness is "a process that takes time for most. When betrayal and miscommunication inhibit our ability to forgive, it's ok to feel those feelings" (and even necessary). "Shock and anger often comes before forgiveness. We must first deal with the hurt feelings before moving into forgiveness."

I liked Dr. Khoddam's findings so much that I integrated them with findings from a Johns Hopkins Psychiatrist,

Dr. Karen Swartz, and created an Anger/Forgiveness Comparison table below including the respective physical associations with each.

Which side of the chart do you want to be on?

Forgive	Stay Angry
• Decrease depression, anxiety and stress • Have more satisfied relationships • Strengthen parenting alliance • Lower white blood cell count (associated with fighting off infection and disease) • Lower risk of heart attack • Improve cholesterol levels and sleep • Reduce pain	• Increase heart rate, blood pressure, stress and immune response • Increase risk of depression, heart disease, diabetes and more! • Increase likeliness of post-traumatic stress disorder

Dr. Deepak Chopra, integrates traditional Western medicine with traditional Eastern health practices, and had the following exchange through a Q & A session with one of his followers.

Excerpt from
Reawakening Lost Energy In Ask Deepak[10]

Question:

"...I work as a nurse practitioner in the community and am a busy mother and wife. At age 53, I feel like I am fading away-my physical my emotional and my spiritual energies. Despite my understanding of foundation of health, I cannot seem to return to a sense of vitality... How does one forgive and forget the awful things you have done in life? What do you think is one or two of the most important things to do to feel better physically?"

Deepak's Answer:

"You brought up the point about how to forgive yourself for the things you regret in your past. That is relevant because holding on to blame and self-recrimination will drain you of physical energy just as effectively as an illness. Start your forgiveness process by recognizing that there was no absolute right or wrong decision to be made. You did the best you knew, based on your understanding at the time. That is all anyone can do. Those choices have led you to this present moment and this is where your current choices lie. This moment is where you can live your life and exercise your power..."

NEXT STEP – PRACTICE RAIN AND ADD "S"

One of my favorite meditation teachers is Dr. Tara Brach, former Psychotherapist, who teaches her students RAIN as part of a Mindfulness Meditation practice. It's

---

10 Reawakening Lost Energy In Ask Deepak. (2018, July 22). Retrieved from The Chopra Center.

a very sweet and thoughtful process that was originally created by Michelle McDonald nearly 20 years ago as a mindfulness tool. More good news about this process is that you don't need to practice mindfulness meditation in order to walk yourself through it.

Here's what the acronym stands for:

1. **Recognize** What is Happening.
2. **Allow** Life to Be Just as It Is.
3. **Inquire** (originally investigate) with Kindness.
4. **Nurture** (originally non-identification) with Self-Compassion.
5. (Adding) a **Shift** will Occur.

I add an "S" at the end because by that time, a shift will have likely occurred, and given a shift, a sense of relief, freedom and wisdom will also follow.

Keeping this in mind, you have many ways to become more resilient, so do whatever you can to release negativity, other people's energy and past experiences that no longer serve you.

Photo by Mick Schultz, MixPix.

Putting RAIN(S) into practice, I've adapted a brief step by step guide from Tara Brach's article, "Ancient Buddhist Way to Cope With Hardship: RAIN is a Buddhist mindfulness tool that offers support for working with intense and difficult emotions.[11]"

1. **Recognize What is Happening**

   Recognition is seeing what is true in your inner life. It starts the minute you focus your attention on whatever thoughts, emotions, feelings, or sensations are arising right here and now. Focus inward and try to let go of preconceived ideas. Listen in a kind, receptive way to your body and heart.

2. **Allow Life to Be Just as It Is**

   Allowing means 'letting be' the thoughts, emotions, feelings, or sensations you discover. You may feel a natural sense of aversion or wish that unpleasant feelings would go away, but as you become more willing to be present with 'what is,' a different quality of attention will emerge. Offer the phrase gently and patiently, and in time your defenses will relax, and you may feel a physical sense of opening to waves of experience.

3. **Investigate with Kindness**

   Inquiry or Investigation means calling on your natural interest—the desire to know truth—and directing a more focused attention to your present experience. You might ask yourself, "How am I

11 Brach, T. (2013, February). Ancient Buddhist Way to Cope With Hardship: RAIN is a Buddhist mindfulness tool that offers support for working with intense and difficult emotions, *Yoga Journal*.

experiencing this in my body?" or "What does this feeling want from me?" Unless they are brought into consciousness, these beliefs and emotions will control your experience and perpetuate your identification with a limited, deficient sense of self. We need to offer a gentle welcome to whatever surfaces.

4. **Nurture with Self-Compassion**

   To do this, try to sense what the wounded, frightened or hurting place inside you most needs and then offer some gesture of active care that might address this need. Does it need a message of reassurance? Of love? Experiment and see which intentional gesture of kindness most helps to comfort, soften or open your heart. It might be the mental whisper, *I'm here with you. I love you. It's not your fault*. Trust in your goodness.

The result of RAIN? We realize we "are no longer imprisoned in the trance of unworthiness, or in any limiting sense of self." This is the "S" or "Shift" I refer to.

When you put RAIN(S) into practice, Tara also recommends that we:

5. **Pause** beforehand to set your intention.
6. **Cultivate flexibility** for your own unique situation.
7. **Seek help** if your personal experience is too intense to go through alone.
8. **Be mindful of doubt** to determine what is healthy doubt vs. doubt that may impede your healing process.

9. **Be patient** because you may need to practice RAIN a number of times to see and feel results.
10. **Practice with the "small stuff"** so you can strengthen the practice itself for the "bigger stuff."

Burn the Pages

You're dark grey like a storm cloud
Swelling up with rage that is desperate to be let out
And I know it's a heavy load carrying those tears around
Carrying those fears around,
worry makes the world go round
You're twisted up like a slipknot
Tied by a juicehead who just took his t-shot, and I know
There's a hungry dog tugging at your frayed ends
But he's just playing with you, he just wants to be your friend
So don't worry, don't worry I'm here by your side
By your side, by your side
We're letting go tonight!
Yesterday is gone and you will be OK
Place your past into a book
Burn the pages, let 'em cook oh
Yesterday is dead and gone and so today
Place your past into a book
Burn the pages, let 'em cook
Eyes stinging from the black smoke, new hope, loose rope
Risen from the undertow, all is well
We welcome the cry, of the dark night sky
Swallow me peacefully, follow my heart back inside
So don't worry, don't worry I'm here by your side
By your side, by your side
We're letting go tonight!
Yesterday is gone and you will be OK
Place your past into a book
Burn the pages, let 'em cook oh
Yesterday is dead and gone and so today
Place your past into a book
Burn the pages, let 'em cook...

- Sia

#forgivenessliberatesus

"Mind you -
The first thing to mind is your mind.

The last thing to mind is your mind."
                              - Stonepeace

Chapter 5

Meditation. Do it.

In America, general programming tells us to be in control and fill our space with things, even our minds. In the East, it even appears that we are supposed to control our thoughts with meditation, forcing our focus "back to our breath." Although this appears to be a form of control, it's actually at its most extreme, a form of mastery. Meditation is a way for us to slow down, create more space and sit in that space, so that we can gain insight, accept and respond to life in kind and thoughtful ways. Sitting in a lot of space can be very uncomfortable. Imagine sitting with someone in silence when you're not meditating or doing anything else physical together. Awkward, right? Especially if you don't know someone well, you usually try to fill that space with words, TV or something!

So, take that concept one step further. If we're not filling the space or controlling our thoughts, we're just being there allowing things to be as they are. It's a feeling of being present and experiencing pure relaxation, but fear (or whatever else that may be buried) may also naturally come to the surface.

When I was in my mid-20's, I started dating someone who meditated himself. I'd been curious about it, but was never as called to do it as I was in that moment. He talked to me about the kind of meditation he did, which was called Vipassana or Insight Meditation. At the time, he had been to several retreats that lasted up to a month (10-day and one-month-long retreats being the most common). I laughed at the idea of going on a month-long retreat, but started by just sitting and breathing. I'd sit for 10 minutes or so once or twice a week, and although it felt really awkward, I just kept at it.

Nearly 20 years later, and after several workshops and retreats, I meditate now every day (for at least 30 minutes) and sometimes twice, if the day has been difficult.

This is what meditation helps me cultivate:

- Self-acceptance and acceptance of others.
- Compassion for self and others.
- Clarity about people and situations – in both my private and professional lives.
- Emotional/psychological/energetic freedom.
- Mastery over my own thoughts, feelings and actions, which includes a shift from knee-jerk reactions to more thoughtful responses.

Now, I:

- Can see things more clearly.
- Am more grounded.
- Have greater awareness of where that boundary is between others and myself.
- Feel more relaxed and connected to myself and others.
- Can see bullshit really easily and tell when people lie to me.

- Am able to focus in meetings and do better work, especially work that requires attention to detail.
- Have a greater sense of well-being, as though everything will be okay.
- Really see the humor in myself and situations.

It's like a natural, magical practice that leads to greater peace, wisdom and happiness!

Addressing negative thought loops

Another thing I've noticed recently, is when I experience the beginning of a repetitive negative thought loop, I will also observe that my mind wants to attach itself to that thought or experience, which will then start another thought loop. I've been meditating so long that I see this and slow down reaction time. Rather than hop onto another train of thought, I just practice continuing to breathe and be in the (what I'll call) "unknowingness" – like you don't know what thought is coming next and you just allow it to be that way. This experience is in direct opposition to the tendency to search for something familiar or try to control where our mind or feelings go next. Mind you, this whole process happens in less than a second. Here is an illustration of what this experience is like:

Beginning of breath   space   thought

----

0 seconds   →   1 second

THE SCIENCE BEHIND IT

What is meditation?

There are a number of meditation practices going back thousands of years. In this section, I focus primarily on a type called Vipassana, which means to see things as they really are. It was taught in India more than 2,500 years ago as a remedy for universal ills..."[12]. Vipassana is also referred to as "Insight Meditation" and most popularly as "Mindfulness Meditation."

Not many people understand the gravity and power of meditation. Deborah Ward[13] states that meditation is "not a religion or a philosophy but a technique that encourages acceptance, appreciation and living in the moment...Mindfulness techniques have even been used in the treatment of depression, anxiety disorders, substance abuse and other health conditions."

People in my own meditation community refer to it as "the practice of loving awareness."

Your brain and neuroscience

Meditation has also been associated with numerous parts of the brain, everywhere from the prefrontal cortex to the brainstem and throughout its gray and white matter.

12 Dhamma.org, retrieved from https://www.dhamma.org/en-US/index.
13 Ward, D. (2014, May). How Mindfulness Can Benefit Highly Sensitive People. *Psychology Today.*

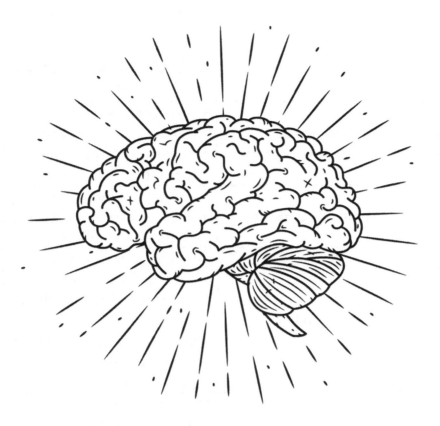

In her article, "The Neuroscience of Mindfulness Meditation," Neuroscientist and Author, Sarah McKay, cites a meta-analysis by the National Center for Biotechnology Information[14] that found eight brain regions consistently altered in experienced meditators. In the table below, I outline a description of those eight regions and what they represent.

---

14 McKay, S. (n.d.). The Neuroscience of Mindfulness Meditation. *The Chopra Center.*

Meditation Affects Eight Regions of the Brain

Part of Brain	What it's Associated With
1. **Rostrolateral prefrontal cortex**	Self-awareness, introspection and the processing of complex information
2. **Sensory cortices**	Auditory, visual, olfactory, and touch sensations and physical awareness
3. **Insular cortex**	Internal and external awareness and the regulation of the body's homeostasis (e.g. compassion and empathy, perception, motor control, cognitive functioning)
4. **Hippocampus**	The center of emotion, memory, and the autonomic nervous system
5. **Anterior cingulate cortex**	Autonomic nervous system (e.g. heart rate and blood pressure) and higher-level brain functions (e.g. decision-making, ethics, impulse control and emotion)
6. **Mid-cingulate cortex**	Processes interpersonal experiences

7. **Superior longitudinal fasciculus**	Regulating and prioritizing motor behavior, controls spatial attention and visual information and transfers sensory neurons and pathways that respond to surface and internal changes of the body
8. **Corpus callosum**	Connects the left and right cerebral hemispheres of the brain, enables communication between the two, and is the largest white matter structure in the human brain

It's surprising even to me, a 20-year meditator, how extensive the reach of meditation is.

Meditation affects our health

There have also been a number of studies about how meditation actually affects health and a person's level of stress and depression. In a neurological and cardiovascular study of meditation[15], "wireless sensor technology was used to measure EEG, blood pressure, heart rate and its variability (HRV) in novice and experienced meditators"

---

15 Steinhubl, S., Wineinger, Nathan, Patel, S, Boeldt, D, Mackellar, G, Porter, V, Redmond, J, Muse, E, Nicholson, L, Chopra, D. and Topol, E. (2015, March). Cardiovascular and nervous system changes during meditation. *Frontiers in Human Neuroscience.*

– during meditation. The results? "Meditation produced ... changes, even among novice meditators on the first day." Additionally, "evidence suggests that the autonomic nervous system can be influenced through meditation... through studies of significant changes in central nervous system..." Lastly, "there is adequate evidence of a long-term benefit of a mediation practice for the treatment of high blood pressure."

If it's stress reduction you're looking for, you'll be interested in hearing what Megan Lee from the Harvard Medical School had to say. She claims in her article[16] that "stress has been linked to low immunity to common illnesses such as depression, high blood pressure and heart disease" and that studies funded by the National Institutes of Health show compelling and consistent results on the effects of transcendental meditation and its "reduction in cardiovascular events (heart attacks, stroke or death), significantly less stress and reduced blood pressure."

More on meditation and stress reduction

In an abstract from the *National Center for Biotechnology Information*[17], authors highlight "...the efficacy of meditation programs in improving stress-related outcomes...in diverse adult clinical populations...After studying over 3,500 participants, Mindfulness Meditation

---

16 Lee, M. Harvard Medical School. (2009, December). Calming Your Nerves and Your Heart Through Meditation. *Science in the News.*
17 Meditation programs for psychological stress and well-being: a systematic review and meta-analysis by Goyal, Singh, Sibinga, Gould, Rowland-Seymour, Sharma, Berger, Sleicher, Maron, Shihab, Ranasinghe, Linn, Saha, Bass, Haythornthwaite, *National Center for Biotechnology Information*, March 2014.

programs had evidence of improved anxiety, depression and pain in two months and then again between three-six months."

-And if you think meditation calms you down just as a vacation would, think again. In an article published in *Translational Psychiatry*[18], authors describe a study on women to test this theory. One month after the six-day study, all three groups of women had "improvements in depressive symptoms, perceived stress, mindful awareness and vitality," so what's the difference you say? For one, the "novice meditators showed greater maintenance of lower distress over time compared to those on the vacation arm." Even 10 months after the study, novice meditators "showed greater decreases in depressive symptoms and stress levels" than their vacationing counterparts. The authors also "identified a 'meditation effect' within the regular meditator group characterized by...cellular functions that may be relevant to healthy aging..."

Meditation and breathing

Now that we have some idea of how meditation affects our brain, our behavior and our wellbeing, let's address the breathing part. We know that breathing is necessary, but it's also central to meditation. New meditators will often ask questions like, "Do I breathe through my nose or mouth?" and "Which one do I breathe in with and which one do I breathe out with?" I was taught to

18 Epel, Puterman, Blackburn, Lum, Beckmann, Zhu, Lee, Gilbert, Rissman, Tanzi & Schadt. (2016. August). Meditation and vacation effects have an impact on disease-associated molecular phenotypes, *Translational Psychiatry*.

breathe in and out with my nose, but until recently, I had no idea why that was. And because of my chronic sinus issues, I often had difficulty doing it.

Why breathe through your nose?

There is an excellent article in *Gaiam* by Gwen Lawrence[19] where she offers a quite comprehensive description of why it's more beneficial to breathe out of our noses. In brief, I summarize the most compelling reasons we should breathe through our noses:

1. **The nose acts as a filter to clean air before it reaches the inside of your body**. It is "lined with tiny hairs called *cilia*", which "filter, humidify and warm or cool the air (depending on the temperature) before it enters the lungs. It is estimated that cilia protect our bodies against about 20 billion particles of foreign matter every day!"

2. **Breathing through our nose slows us down, has a calming effect and gets more oxygen into our bodies**. "Breathing in and out through the nose helps us take fuller, deeper breaths, which stimulates the lower lung to distribute greater amounts of oxygen throughout the body. Also, the lower lung is rich with the parasympathetic nerve receptors associated with calming the body and mind, whereas the upper lungs — which are stimulated by chest and mouth breathing — prompt us to hyperventilate and trigger sympathetic

19 Lawrence, G. (n.d) Breathing is Believing: The importance of nasal breathing. *Gaiam.*

nerve receptors, which result in the fight or flight reaction."

3. **Exhaling through the nose allows the lungs to process more oxygen**. "Because the nostrils are smaller than the mouth, air exhaled through the nose creates a back flow of air (and oxygen) into the lungs. And because we exhale more slowly through the nose than we do through the mouth, the lungs have more time to extract oxygen from the air we've already taken in."

4. **Mouth breathing can cause snoring and sleep apnea**. "Mouth breathing bypasses the nasal mucosa and makes regular breathing difficult, which can lead to snoring, breath irregularities and sleep apnea."

Fun fact: Lawrence brings to our attention that "In 1931, Otto Warburg won a Nobel Prize for determining that only oxygen-starved cells will mutate and become cancerous." Now, if *that* doesn't scare you into breathing through your nose...

Note about stuffy noses: If you have chronic sinus issues, I encourage you to see a doctor, but as it relates to meditation and/or a stuffy nose during meditation (while you're trying to breathe through your nose), Gwen Lawrence and I both recommend what's called "sinus irrigation." Since I have sinus issues myself, I use what's called a Sinus Rinse. It's the easiest. However, you can also use a Neti Pot or any number of other tools that can be found on the internet or by walking into a drug or grocery store.

As an HSP

Meditation is not only a very natural practice for the HSP, since, as Deborah Ward states[20], the "HSP experiences the world in essentially a mindful way...", but it also balances the intensity of feelings we experience (of both ourselves and others) by creating enough time, peace and space for us to pay attention to our own needs. "The key facets of mindfulness can help us to be an HSP while creating a life that is calm, peaceful and happy..." She adds (and I agree) that "taking time for solitude, for downtime, for creative time, for taking walks in nature is essential for the well-being of HSPs."

Dr. Elaine Aron makes a powerful statement when she says that "simply closing your eyes removes 80% of the stimulation to your brain."[21] This is good news for the overstimulated HSP. And if you find it challenging to put time aside for meditation, know that the time spent in quiet silence or solitude is "made up for by feeling fresh, tranquil, and efficient when you do work." Lastly, the quick acting HSP benefits from the deep reflection of meditation and "previous quiet thought."

---

20 Ward, D. (2014, May). How Mindfulness Can Benefit Highly Sensitive People. *Psychology Today.*
21 Aron, E, PhD. (2018, February). *The Power of Inner Silence for HSPs.* Retrieved from https://hsperson.com/the-power-of-inner-silence-for-hsps.

An HSP with meditation in action

Being quiet in your mind is not just about sitting in solitude, however. It's about the way we engage in life. As an example, being in traffic is usually stressful for everyone, not just an HSP, but it can be even more so for the HSP. And let me tell you, it is stressful for me! Point being, through years of meditation, I'm able to (when consciously aware) sit in gridlock traffic and simply focus on my breathing. Strangely, when I do this for longer than a few minutes, the traffic sometimes even lightens and opens up. It's almost as if letting go of my own attachment to outcome opens things up inside of me and then ripples outward. But the thing is, when I'm fully present and breathing, I don't feel stressed. It feels as if I'm distracting myself from myself with my breath.

In the case of being cut off my someone or close to getting in an accident, I practice a similar internal process. Almost 100% of the time, I'll have an immediate fear or anger response, but again, when in a mindful place, I allow myself to emotionally react – as in feeling the anger and fear and taking slow, deep breaths. By doing so, the feelings surface and then move on and I'm at equilibrium again. This is very powerful stuff, particularly for an HSP!

Next Step – How to Meditate

Photo by Mick Schultz, MixPix.

Just sit and focus on your breath. It's pretty much as easy as that! If you need more direction, feel free to follow the tips I've outlined below, which represent what I've learned over the years:

1. Think of a time of day when you can spare a little bit of extra time and/or when in the day you feel most stressed. This can be when you first wake up, after work or even on public transportation to and from work!

2. Carve out at least 10 minutes during that time- even if it's one day a week.

3. Find a sacred space in your home or in a quiet, private and safe place outside of your home. If this is difficult, remember the comment about public transportation.

4. Get a meditation pillow or comfortable chair to sit on (you don't have to be uncomfortable and/

or sit in the lotus position in order to meditate effectively).

5. Be still, but if you have to move, be present with whatever movement you need to make.

6. Try to sit as "erect" as possible – where your back is straight, shoulders are down and you're slightly engaging your stomach muscles.

7. Close your eyes or keep them slightly open with a downward gaze (if you tend to fall asleep).

8. Start to watch and hear your breathing.

9. When you notice that your mind wanders, notice it and gently refocus your attention to your breath.

10. If you find you are having repetitive thoughts or feelings (e.g. repetitive thoughts over a previous mistake at work or in a relationship, etc.), observe the pattern as a witness and simply allow the thought or feeling to be there. Watch it and breathe. Consider going through the RAIN(S) practice mentioned in Chapter 4 on Forgiveness.

11. When you notice that you're distracted by a sensation in your body, observe the sensation and where it's located, and gently refocus your attention to your breathing. If you have repetitive sensations in your body (e.g. tight throat; tight tummy, etc.), you may want to treat that as a repetitive thought (see above) – allowing it to be there without judgment. Again, consider going through the RAIN(S) practice mentioned in Chapter 4 on Forgiveness.

12. Keep going.

There! You've just meditated!

Regarding steps 9 through 11 above: when you observe repetitive thoughts and/or sensations in your body, they may either be released through the process of breathing into them or by neutral acceptance and observation. By following the RAIN(S) practice, you can learn more about what's bothering you to gain insight.

Really important: You will be distracted often. Expect this to happen. The tendency is to be judgmental about getting distracted, but distraction is a natural part of the practice. 1) You may also learn from your distractions and 2) by refocusing your mind on your breathing, you're strengthening your consciousness muscle – your ability to manage (not control) your mind. Essentially, you're making yourself smarter!

Warning: Doing this also reveals who you are to yourself. This may change your self-perception and a realization of your true values, which may then lead to a change in professions and/or relationships.

Lovesong

Whenever I'm alone with you
You make me feel like I am home again
Whenever I'm alone with you
You make me feel like I am whole again...
Whenever I'm alone with you
You make me feel like I am free again
Whenever I'm alone with you
You make me feel like I am clean again...

– The Cure

#meditationismagic

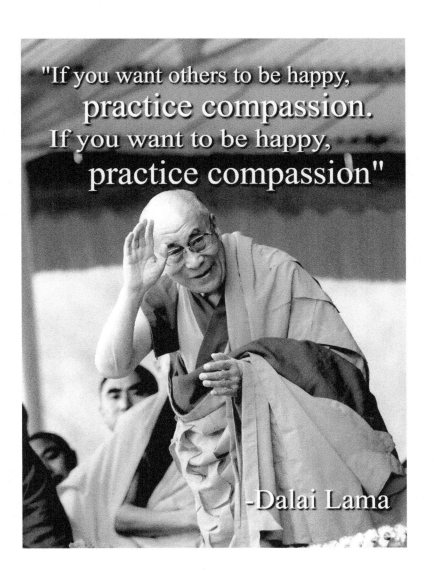

Chapter 6

Loving yourself is a practice. Practice it.

Love has many forms. It is a verb, a noun and can even be used as an adjective (e.g. when a person is lovable, etc.). Even though love is often referred to in a noun-type of context, I'd like to focus on love as a verb – an action – a practice. So, what does that look like?

Love as self-care

For my body, I go to the gym, run or do yoga. For my mind, I meditate, do energy work and visualizations, and pray. Self-care – physical and mental - can also take many forms. I had a reading from an intuitive once, and he told me that I "wouldn't like what he was about to tell me." I had just turned 30 you see and was still into sleeping in past 11:00 AM, staying out late, experimenting with drugs, etc. – yet was still moving on a path of greater awareness and psychological health. He gingerly went on to say that I'd "need to practice some form of energy work every day." At the time, I had been meditating for over five years, but didn't have a regular practice.

He was right; I didn't like hearing that, but I now agree it's true. I meditate or practice self-Reiki once a day and sometimes twice on bad days or when I feel I really need it. But it doesn't stop there! I've also learned that I need to exercise multiple times a week and am happiest when I'm also having sex several times a week. It's a lot of work! Clearly, I don't have children, but if that situation should change, I'd need to create a new routine to maintain balance and self-care.

Self-care also means that you respect and trust yourself. This manifests in the boundaries you set with people and how you communicate with them and about yourself (refer to Chapter 7: Get Yourself Some Boundaries). Are you using kind words when you describe yourself? Do you receive compliments? Do you take time to make decisions?

Love as joy

But self-care doesn't just mean you work hard on yourself. It also means that you do things that make you happy – daily. For me now, what I look forward to during the day is either 1) going home to relax in front of Netflix with a "nightcap" 2) meeting a friend or two+ for happy hour or brunch or 3) spending time with loved ones. Previously, I'd go on dates too, but for the most part, they were more a form of stress and an investment of energy, in hopes that it would yield positive results in the long run.

Another way I've learned to love myself is through laughter and doing so often – even if it's at myself. I find that being able to laugh at situations and myself makes it easier to take things less seriously. I mean, the immediate result of laughter is joy obviously, but it really gets energy moving and helps me appreciate situations for their irony and at times, absurdity. It also allows me to hear things that may be difficult, like during times when I need to work with others to make work the best it can be or when I'm being intimate with family, friends or a romantic partner.

Having fun, laughing, being with loved ones, relaxing – all of these things bring me joy and balance to hard work. I recommend you find what those things are for you and do whatever brings a smile to your face often!

Sitting with discomfort is a form of love

If you're afraid of your feelings, sit with your fear; watch it, breathe into it. It's okay to be angry; it's okay to feel sad and express these feelings. Being with any feeling that comes up is a very basic and primary way to love and accept yourself. By allowing them to be there and holding them in gentle kindness, watch/observe the feelings as you would a witness. Sometimes the feelings will change. Sometimes you need to imagine the feelings growing outward as if they're moving or expanding through your body until they evaporate or fall away. This is a practice recommended by Dr. Deepak Chopra.

As an example, when I sit with uncomfortable thoughts and/or feelings, I imagine that I'm holding a sacred, gentle, kind space for them to exist. Almost as if I were allowing space for someone I loved to feel what they needed to feel or being present for someone who is in distress. The same way we hold an animal we love, a child or other loved one. I literally imagine holding that energy, thought or emotion in the same way. In my mind, this is a form of pure self-care, love and acceptance. I find that when I'm able to just allow feelings to be (however dark – the darker, the more important this exercise), 1) the more quickly they move outside of my space 2) the more grounded and connected I feel and 3) the more I'm left with an overall sense of joy, self-acceptance and self-love. Conversely, while in this mode, I also happen to be in a pretty consistent state of discomfort. It's challenging and requires conscious effort – like a mental exercise. This practice also softens edges overall and when you're able to do this for yourself, it translates into your ability to do it for others.

It's through practices like these that I'm able to truly accept myself, loving even the darkest, scariest parts.

Here are some mantras that can help on your journey of continued self-love:

- "I don't need a man to be whole."
- "I don't need a relationship to be worthy."
- "I am whole and worthy as I am now."

...And some healthy life principles and practices:

- Practice self-care each day.
- Don't make yourself smaller to make others more comfortable.
- Don't apologize for who you are.
- Don't let other people define you.
- Honor your own voice even if you're afraid.
- Say kind things to yourself.
- Speak your truth.
- Own your shit.
- Command your own power.
- Choose the stories you tell yourself.
- Be your own advocate.
- Be your own best friend.

- Love yourself.
- Remember that love is a verb, an adjective and a noun.

An HSP?

Self-love may be a bit more challenging, since our insula is more active than others (refer to Chapter 1: Highly Sensitive People: Are you one of them?). This increased sense of self-awareness can lead to self-criticism and inhibition, as well as, the general sense that we're different than others. The good news for an HSP, however, is that when positive practices are adopted, they are more likely to have a greater impact. So practice, practice, practice!

Photo by Mick Schultz, MixPix.

THE SCIENCE BEHIND IT

How do the experts define self-love? Dr. John Amodeo, licensed Marriage and Family Therapist, writes[22] that

22 Amodeo, J. PhD, MFT. (2015, October). What It Really Means to Love Yourself. *Psychology Today.*

"self-love means finding peace within ourselves"... having "empathy and unconditional positive regard for whatever we are experiencing inside." He refers to self-love as an "antidote to shame" and offers it up as an alternative to "battling ourselves or trying to fix or change ourselves." It's not all rainbows and teddy bears, however. It's very natural and "human to feel sad, hurt, and afraid sometimes. It's a sign of strength, not weakness, to become mindful of these feelings and allow a friendly space for them." (Refer to Chapter 5: Meditation: Do it.).

Deanna Michalopoulos tells a story[23] about a "Type-A woman" who formerly owned six McDonald's franchises. After (among other things) having a realization that 'we're at the mercy of the external world when we launch into the day without plugging into ourselves first', this woman, Barb Schmidt "has forged a mega-mission to help spiritual seekers find happiness within." Schmidt adds that "perspective shifts as you spend more time with yourself. You realize this is the only way to be." As a student of Deepak Chopra and Thich Nhat Hanh, Schmidt has embarked on her own *I Love Me Workshop* and offers a bit of advice for those dedicated to self-love: 'Stop saying yes when you want to say no, and quit running around doing things that don't matter to you because you don't feel complete.'

Serena Chen, Ph.D. and Professor of Psychology at the University of California, Berkeley, suggests that rather than "become defensive and blame others or berate

23 Michalopoulos, D. (2015, February). 10 Ways to Love Yourself (More) in the Modern World. *Yoga Journal.*

ourselves," it's far more effective to "treat ourselves as we would a friend" to "be kind, understanding, and encouraging" and defines this "type of response internally, towards ourselves as self-compassion..." In her *Harvard Business Review* article[24], she primarily focuses on how self-compassion affects people's ability to develop professionally.

Most notably as a researcher of self-compassion, Chen links self-compassion to higher levels of self-esteem and authenticity, and outlines three behaviors that people with high levels of self-compassion typically demonstrate.

1. "They are kind rather than judgmental about their own failures and mistakes,
2. They recognize that failures are a shared human experience, and
3. They take a balanced approach to negative emotions" – allowing themselves to 'feel badly' without being consumed by negative emotions.

Furthermore, Chen says that "treating oneself with kindness, understanding, and without judgment alleviates fears about social disapproval...minimizes negative thoughts and self-doubts...and increases compassion for others."

Next Step - A journaling exercise
I first learned about journaling as a daily practice by reading and participating in exercises in *The Artist's Way* by Julia Cameron, a great book I highly recommend.

---

24 Chen, S. (2018, September/October). Give Yourself a Break: The Power of Self-Compassion. *Harvard Business Review*.

Once through the book, I began journaling as part of my own spiritual and psychological health routine. It's an excellent way to get random thoughts out of your head, clear it up for more creative thinking and allow yourself to work through issues on paper.

The following are great ways to write to yourself in support of self-love. I've borrowed and refined this list from Zen Meditation Teacher, Mary Ellen Hammond's book, *There Is Nothing Wrong With You*. As she says (and I think it's brilliant), "Only you know how you want to be loved and only you can love yourself the way you want and need to be loved."

1. Write down all of those things you've always wanted someone to say to you and add to this list when you think of something else you want to hear.
2. Read this list daily.
3. Make another list of things you'd like to have and begin providing them for yourself.
4. Say thank you to yourself when you do something kind, even (and especially) if the other person did not thank you.
5. While journaling, write down what you say to berate yourself, both internally and to others. Each time you're aware of a new way, remind yourself that you were likely programmed to think this and replace those thoughts and words with love and acceptance.

All Babies

There's only love
There's only love
There's only love in this world
There's only love
There's only love
There's only love in this world
-Sinead O'Connor

#fearisanillusiononlyloveisreal

Meme graphic by iMeme.

Chapter 7

Get Yourself Some Boundaries.

The earliest memory I have of my mother is of her crying. She was in the middle of a divorce with my father. I was about five years old at the time. Feeling her pain, I also remember being in front of her and trying to comfort her, telling her I loved her and that everything would be okay. My mother and I were close growing up, and that behavior of consoling or playing the role of a healer was my first memory of what kind of behavior I thought would bring me love.

I first learned about setting energetic boundaries in my late 20's by doing energy work at a place called Berkeley Psychic Institute (BPI). (Refer to Chapter 2: Energy exists, so don't look at me like that!). As a reminder, BPI's main purpose was to teach people how to create these energetic boundaries to protect themselves against "emotional vampires".

In recent years, I realized that many of the people I've dated also wanted to be healed. The only difference now is that I don't want to be a part of it -- 35 years later! That's how powerful this crap is! *Unbelievable.*

An HSP?
Typically, people who are HSPs and/or who have natural healing abilities struggle with boundaries. Not an HSP?

This can still be difficult, as it seems the world screams at us daily and tells us how to be. Are we becoming the messages we get from the media, our loved ones and people who want something from us?

"Mansplaining"

Yet another form of boundary intrusion is when men talk over women and engage in a recently coined phrase called "Mansplaining". It is defined as a man explaining something to someone (and sometimes *over* someone), typically a woman, in a manner that is condescending or patronizing.

Pervasive in professional settings, men will talk over us, cut us off and tell us what is 'correct' and at times, what we should believe. This is often done with a condescending and/or directive tone. They will either tell us about something they think they know better than we do, or they will merely talk over us altogether. Being in the business world for over 20 years, I've had first-hand experience with this and it gets worse the higher up you are in management. Egos appear boundless. My style tends to be cheerful and "jokey" in general with a focus on factual data, context, short- and long-term implications and general successful outcomes. I will "open a can of whoop ass" on occasion, but only under extreme situations.

When men speak to me in a condescending tone, I will usually respond with the same tone with a half-smile on my face. Sometimes, I will also listen and say, "Uh huh. I hear you and I disagree..." I've also had a number of male colleagues have outbursts in meetings – literally yelling at each other in pure anger. *And they say women are emotional!* I have one colleague in particular who is prone to bits of public rage and condescension, but who actually means well and has important things to say; he just doesn't say them in an effective way. I have privately told him that what he's saying is good, but that because of the way he is delivering the message, people cannot hear it because they cannot get past the harsh tone, etc.

Men "mansplaining" over other men

What's compelling, however, is that after years of observation, I find that men also cut each other off, talk over each other and tell each other what to do and think. The lesson is that it's not necessarily a male/female dynamic; it's more about the male ego, communication style and the lack of listening. And if a woman does not communicate in the same demanding and ego-centered way, the man will just continue with what he's doing with the woman not being heard.

For example, I was in a weekly meeting, and it was my turn to speak. I started speaking and then a person started having a side conversation. A male co-worker of mine in the meeting said, "Heather is speaking; let her finish." The very next week, this same male co-worker was in the middle of reporting back on research he had done, and two people started a side conversation. I then intervened on his behalf and said, "[so and so] is speaking; will you let him finish?" In both cases, those who misbehaved fell silent in response to our pleas for listening.

THE SCIENCE BEHIND IT

The EEOC calls this a "bystander intervention" and both they and James Campbell Quick and M. Ann McFadyen[25] agree that this kind of colleague intervention can help prevent incidences as serious as sexual harassment.

There are always a**holes who target women and/or innately disrespect us because of our gender, but they are far fewer in numbers. Quick and McFadyen "estimate that (a mere) 1% to 3% of individuals within an organization have the potential to become deviant, dysfunctional, or dangerous." My theory is that this behavior is attributed to the fact that most men have a hard time listening, are ego-driven and are more aggressive by nature.

Women don't need to act like men to have boundaries

On a separate yet related note, women do not need to act and communicate in an aggressive manner or like a man to be heard. We can simply exercise different forms of healthy boundaries.

---

25 Quick Campbell, J and McFadyen, Ann M. (2018, February). Bad Behavior Is Preventable, *Harvard Business Review*.

Photo by Mick Schultz, MixPix

Identifying where the boundaries are

In Dr. John Amodeo's article, "What It Means to Create Boundaries in Relationships[26]," he defines the essence of boundaries as "differentiating what we want from what others want from us." In order to understand what we need, he recommends what Tara Brach calls the 'sacred pause,' where we slow down enough to be present with what we're experiencing in the moment. But having healthy boundaries is not just about connecting with our own needs and affirming them. Amodeo clarifies that healthy boundaries mean "entering into a collaborative process with people." By maintaining flexibility and

26 Amodeo, J, PhD. (2018, October). What It Means to Create Boundaries in Relationships. *Psychology Today.*

honoring the other person's needs as well, we can "create a climate for intimate, loving relationships…"

Boundaries have many layers

Psychologist and Yoga Instructor, Bo Forbes, describes boundaries[27] by using the apple as a metaphor. The first and most obvious layer is the skin of the apple, what people see in terms of behavior. An example of this is how much time and effort you offer others vs. how much time and effort you need for yourself. The second layer of the apple "the flesh," which corresponds to the interpersonal, emotional nature of the relationship can be seen "when you feel someone's emotions as though they were your own", and consequently, "may have the urge to relieve their suffering" regardless of "the emotional cost to yourself." The third layer or the "core of the apple" is associated with our *intra*personal relationship, which is how easily we can read and respond to our own internal signals about what those needs and boundaries are. "When we lack boundaries at this level, we often have nervous system imbalances, such as anxiety and depression."

In order to "feel and set boundaries with greater clarity," Forbes recommends working with the "innermost layer out", the apple's core. (In addition to yoga poses), this translates into "present-moment awareness that's felt in the body" and deep nasal breathing, both of which often exist in mindfulness and meditation (refer to Chapter 5: Meditation. Do it.).

---

27 Forbes, B. (2016, June). A Sequence + Meditation for Setting Healthy Boundaries. *Yoga Journal.*

In summary, we've addressed a number of ways that boundaries influence our lives, from working with energy, to communicating and managing our own behavior and mental state.

NEXT STEP – HEALTHY PRACTICES AND TIPS

With that said, here are some healthy life practices:

- Let people own their own crazy.
- Don't get caught up in other people's drama.
- Listen to your inner voice – the quiet, gentle one that serves your highest good. (Meditation helps with this!)
- Don't let people steal your joy.
- Don't let men tell you what's right for you, your work and your body.

At BPI, I also learned about the concept of the rose as a tool for imagery and energetic boundaries. One exercise you can use from this concept is that when someone talks to you and it feels badly, you can imagine a rose to the right of your face or away from your body in some fashion. While the person speaks at you, imagine that what they're saying is passing by you and landing directly into the rose so that you do not absorb their anger or toxic energy.

Other ways you can respond with communication when you are being "railroaded" by a man (or other women):

1. Just keep talking.
2. Speak more loudly and keep going.
3. Put your hand up and keep talking.

4. Say "hold on; let me finish." Use your hand, if needed.

5. Say "wait; I'm not done yet." The hand also works here.

6. Say "[their name], you're interrupting!" You can say this in a half-kidding tone, and still get the point across.

7. When you're listening to someone who consistently interrupts you, tell him/her "This is what listening looks like. I'm not interrupting you; I'm listening quietly to what you're saying." You can also say this in a gentle, half-joking tone and the message should be received.

8. If this problem becomes a pattern with any one person, you can also speak to them privately and let them know it bothers you, but only if you feel safe and have a good rapport with them.

9. And if a man (or woman for that matter) uses your idea as their own, feel free to say, "Hey, that was my idea!" As usual, when your tone is more light-hearted, your message will be easier to receive.

Human Nature

...And I'm not sorry
It's human nature
And I'm not sorry
I'm not your bitch don't hang your shit on me
You punished me for telling you my fantasies
I'm breakin' all the rules I didn't make
You took my words and made a trap for silly fools
You held me down and tried to make me break
Did I say something true?
Oops, I didn't know I couldn't talk about sex
Did I have a point of view?
Oops, I didn't know I couldn't talk about you
And I'm not sorry
It's human nature
And I'm not sorry
I'm not your bitch don't hang your shit on me
Express yourself, don't repress yourself
Express yourself, don't repress yourself
Express yourself, don't repress yourself
Express yourself, don't repress yourself...

- Madonna

#bekindandtakenoshit

"...Fall in love with as many things as possible."

- Gwyneth Paltrow as Kelly Canter in Country Song

Chapter 8

Gratitude is more than you think, and I think you'll like it.

Gratitude is a beautiful, very powerful thing. Yet with so much negativity and over-sensationalism bombarding us daily, it's sometimes difficult to remember all of those gifts that we have. If you follow monotheistic religions like Christianity, you are taught to give thanks at times, such as before you eat. As children, most of us are also instructed to thank loved ones and those in our community for gifts given and acts of kindness. In both cases, although it's positive to have a ritual of gratitude and practice manners, these signs of gratitude can feel obligatory and mechanical. There is a difference between when we are socially expected to do something vs. when we feel appreciation in our heart and body.

So, what is gratitude really? The dictionary defines it as "the quality of being thankful; readiness to show appreciation for and to return kindness."

As I see it, there are three primary forms of gratitude:

1. What we project externally towards people in our personal and professional lives when they have done something kind for us;
2. What we feel internally for those positive things we have in our lives; and

3. A spiritual practice that also opens us up to attract more of the same.

As an HSP who struggles with depression, yet likes to spread positivity, I can tell you it's much easier to project gratitude externally, both in personal and professional relationships, than it is to do the latter.

However, lately I've been feeling a shift away from the "negativity and over-sensationalism bombarding us daily" by way of consciously refocusing on all in my life that I find beautiful and feel love for. I've been told for years to practice gratitude, but unless I feel something as an authentic experience, I'm rarely able to practice it. My "ah ha" moment came when I started posting "Daily Beauties" and "Daily Loves" on social media.

Over the weeks of doing this daily, it has expanded to me finding and sharing things that are also hilarious, intelligent and wise. Being a visual artist and a romantic, it's easy for me to see beauty and feel love for people, things, causes, so I started there. My thought was, *what if I just focused on those things and shared them, almost as an anecdote to the often hellacious nature of what we're exposed to in the media?* I then wrote down a list of all of those things that I loved and the list grew quickly. What became apparent at that point, per the growing list and all of these images of beauty and humor, was that abundance exists in my life, and with no effort, I naturally felt and continued to feel gratitude.

THE SCIENCE BEHIND IT

Being a spiritual person, I'm often told by spiritual teachers and other practitioners to use gratitude to attract abundance. But what about Western science?

In my effort to learn more, I found that there have been quite a lot of studies done on gratitude. Physiologically, "when people are consciously grateful, they receive a wave of reward by neurotransmitters, such as dopamine, and experience an alerting and brightening of the mind."[28]

How gratitude manifests in behavior

How this manifests in behavior has also been measured in a number of studies. In just two articles in *Psychology Today* and *Harvard Health Publishing* (out of the Harvard Medical School), there were 10 studies referenced, which cited consistently positive results. Although the results were correlational in nature (as opposed to showing a cause and effect relationship between gratitude and a positive outcome), the patterns were clear.

Psychotherapist and Author, Amy Morin, references Robert Emmons, a leading gratitude researcher, who states that "gratitude effectively increases happiness and reduces depression." She also refers to "a 2006 study when Vietnam War veterans with higher levels of gratitude experienced lower rates of post-traumatic stress disorder" and "a 2003 study... that found that gratitude was a major contributor to resilience following the terrorist attacks on September 11."

---

28 Hampton, D. (2018, January). How Your Thoughts Change Your Brain. *The Best Brain Possible.*

A number of other studies were cited in an article, "In Praise of Gratitude" by *Harvard Health Publishing*. In one, a Psychologist at the University of Pennsylvania, Dr. Martin E.P. Seligman, "tested the impact of various positive psychology interventions on 411 people... When their week's assignment was to write and personally deliver a letter of gratitude to someone who had never been properly thanked for his or her kindness, participants immediately exhibited a huge increase in happiness scores. This impact was greater than that from any other intervention, with benefits lasting for a month."

Gratitude can increase productivity

In yet another one cited in this publication, researchers at the University of Pennsylvania divided university fundraisers into two groups. In one group, the fundraisers solicited donations in the same way they always had. The second group received a pep talk from their Director before soliciting donations. She told the second group that she was grateful for their efforts. "During the following week, the university employees who heard her message of gratitude made 50% more fundraising calls than those who did not."

Summary of the benefits of gratitude

From the research, Amy Morin summarizes the results in the following seven scientifically proven benefits. I added one to make eight!

Gratitude:

1. Opens the door to more relationships.

2. Improves physical health.
3. Improves psychological health.
4. Enhances empathy and reduces aggression.
5. Helps people sleep better.
6. Improves self-esteem.
7. Increases mental strength.
8. (I've added!) Enhances motivation.

Photo by Mick Schulz, MixPix.

NEXT STEP – 8 WAYS TO FEEL AND EXPRESS GRATITUDE (IN AN AUTHENTIC WAY)

1. Slow down and start noticing the beauty that surrounds you. I'm talking about all of the beautiful trees that line the freeways while you're driving in traffic. Also, while in traffic, check out the beautiful blue sky and the clouds that appear to be perfectly painted there as if in a piece of art.
2. While eating and drinking things you really love, be present with it. Savor and appreciate it.

3. Journal or write down all of those things in your life and out in the world that you love. Look at how long the list is, and add to the list as things come up for you. See the list continue to grow. While you're at it, give thanks for those things listed.

4. Think about people in your life who you love and appreciate. Tell them you love and appreciate them!

5. Give someone a compliment each day.

6. When someone does something kind for you, thank them with earnestness and enthusiasm!

7. Write a letter of gratitude to an individual who did something nice for you and has not been adequately thanked yet. Note: You do not need to send the letter, and the person can even be deceased.

8. If you need help at work, thank that person in advance for their time, especially in an email or text.

Gratitude

...Just one thing, do you know you?
What you think, that the world owes you?
What's gonna set you free?
Look inside and you'll see
When you've got so much to say it's called gratitude
And that's right

-Beastie Boys

#themoreyoulovethemoreyoureceive

Meme graphic by iMeme.

Chapter 9

Ask for what you need. It's okay.

Let's face it ladies; many of us secretly want things a certain way, yet we are not direct about it. We may not believe we're worthy of having our needs met, and in the meantime, people around us will sense something is wrong and are generally confused by our silence. But what if we *are* worthy? What if people around us need direction about what's going on in our head and heart?

I've spent many years not wanting to bother people, just worrying about meeting their needs and staying under the radar for the sake of safety. As someone who likes to please others (and who can read what they want), I would often give and give, and not ask for my needs to be met in return. This would often lead me to feel resentful and barren – like an empty carcass.

But now after 40+ years of life (and to depict a less graphic visual), I've learned how to better navigate giving and receiving and goal setting. Even though I don't like bothering people, including asking them for money (even though my current 9-5 job is in marketing-communications), I understand that in some situations it's necessary, and because it's not a strength of mine, I realize it's best to ask for help. While working on this book, a girlfriend of mine told me how much it cost her to write her own book (alarming!) and that a friend of hers had raised money with a crowdfunding campaign. Now knowing that people did this and that I am apprehensive to ask for money, I hired this person who had successfully done it herself and had her coach me through the process and hold me accountable. The result? We were able to raise enough money to cover a third of the book's expenses, and by reaching out to thousands of people, also raised awareness about the book.

If you are an HSP, you may be especially unclear on what your needs are – given the tendency to be overtaken (and overwhelmed) by other's feelings and shutting down. In this case, meditation and energy work are great options for you in clarifying where those boundaries are (refer to two chapters: Meditation. Do it. and Get Yourself Some Boundaries.).

Whether you are an HSP or not, there are a number of situations where asking for what you need (and want) is important, such as in personal relationships, your job or career, creative projects and life goals.

THE SCIENCE BEHIND IT

By researching how the experts address this issue, I found that the best way to get your needs met is to follow both an internal and external process, and that the approach is different depending on whether you're in a personal or professional situation.

Let's first examine the internal process.

Signs you're not getting your needs met

As women, we are so used to being told how to feel and how to think and what to do with our bodies – whether it's personal hygiene, medical advice, what to buy, how to look, and who to have sex with, etc. Because there is so much information coming at us from the external world (that is dominated by men), it can be difficult to even know what our needs are and how to read our own feelings.

As Margie Warrell[29] puts it in her *Forbes* article, there are a number of signs that indicate your needs are not being met:

- You start feeling overwhelmed and/or resentful.
- You find yourself wishing someone would stop doing something you don't like or start doing something you do like.
- You feel underappreciated for your time, contribution or opinion.
- You feel cheated.

Warrell says, "If you find yourself wrestling with any of those emotions, chances are you aren't asking enough of those around you (or are asking ineffectually)."

Now that you know how to identify that the needs aren't being met, you need to look more deeply, reframe the situation and identify what it is that you truly desire. It's helpful to understand that, as Clinical Psychologist, Ellen Hendriksen puts it in her article in the *Scientific American*[30], "people love helping. Not only does helping

---

29 Warrell, M. (2013, April). 7 Keys To Asking For What You Really Want (So You Get It!). *Forbes*.
30 Hendriksen, E. (2014, May). How to Ask for Help. *Scientific American*.

strengthen social ties, it makes helpers feel good about themselves. The most primitive part of the brain – the same reward pathway activated by food and sex – lights up in response to altruistic giving." In identifying what you need, also "ask yourself, what are you no longer willing to tolerate?".

And don't question whether you deserve something or not. Simply focus on what it is you want, so you can increase your chances of getting it.

How to know what your needs are

In her article[31], quoting podcast host Jenna Kutcher, Erika Prafder addresses goal setting by "identifying your ambitions, setting deadlines, surrounding yourself with supportive people and refusing to listen to self-limiting beliefs." Kutcher, a 30-year old self-made millionaire and yogi, says we start by having "limiting beliefs of what we're capable of [and] allow a negative inner narrative to come true."

We must first manage our "thoughts and the way [we] speak to [ourselves] about what [we] believe to be possible," she explains. "To get at the root of what [we] really want rather than what society has influenced [us] to strive for, try asking 'Why?' – and then asking again. This self-inquiry helps [us] dig deeper and create goals [we're] truly excited about and can follow through on."

There is also a distinction yet connection between asking for what we need, getting those needs met and achieving goals. By actively setting goals, we take this

31 Prafder, E. (2018, October). 10 Things Most of us Don't Do When Trying to Achieve a Goal – But Should. *Yoga Journal.*

concept a step further and bring even more of what we want into our lives.

When setting those goals, Kutcher recommends:

- Prioritizing [our] top three goals.
- Sharing [our] goals with others.
- Not competing with other women -- understanding that their success is just a reflection of what's possible for [us].

To balance our wants, it's also important to be "realistic in [our] expectations," as pointed out by Barton Goldsmith Ph.D.[32]. "Lowering [our] expectations is not the same as making them realistic... It's healthier to have preferences rather than expectations, that way [we] won't feel as disappointed if your preference isn't met."

Furthermore, "sometimes our needs (and wants) can be in direct opposition to someone else's." When this happens, "it's important to remember to balance healthy self-assertion with consideration and respect for others," says Alexandra Latos in her article, *How to Ask for What You Want and Need (No, It's Not Selfish).*[33] She adds, "There are times to stand [our] ground and times to compromise, and the trick is to learn to tell the difference."

In a professional context, "women have a harder time than men at asking for what they want when it comes to salaries. Studies of women who are reluctant to ask for

32 Goldsmith, B. Ph.D. (2013, January). 10 Ways to Get Your Emotional Needs Met: Tips to heal your love-life, *Psychology Today.*
33 Latos, A. How to Ask for What You Want and Need (No, It's Not Selfish). *Tiny Buddha.*

pay raises show that they feel that deep down, they aren't deserving of a higher salary.", says Professor Emerita of Psychological and Brain Sciences, Susan Krauss Ph.D.[34]

In the case of negotiating a salary or raise, look up how others are being paid in your industry, geographic location and with your credentials. This data is referred to as your "market value". Two resources you can use to find this information are Glassdoor.com and payscale.com. Do the research. It will give you a reality check, validate your skills, gifts and knowledge, and give you a strong basis on which to stand during the negotiation process. And once you know what your "market value" is, add 10% for negotiation room. Also, be ready to walk away. You increase your leverage by having at least one other job offer as well, so keep your options open before you take a job or before you consider asking for a raise. Lastly, negotiate hardest before being hired. It's far more difficult to negotiate once you're employed.

How to communicate about those needs (and have them met)

Now that we've explored the internal process, let's address behaviors.

Personally

In an article put out by the American Psychological Association[35] on how to keep relationships healthy, "researchers have found that communication style is more important than commitment levels, personality

34 Whitbourne, Krauss S, Ph.D., (2012, December). 9 Ways to Ask For (and Get) What You Want. *Psychology Today.*
35 Haight, R. PsyD. and Abrahamson, D. PhD. Happy couples: How to keep your relationship healthy. *American Psychological Association.*

traits or stressful life events in predicting whether happily married couples will go on to divorce. In particular, negative communication patterns, such as anger and contempt are linked to an increased likelihood of splitting up." So try your hardest to avoid such things "as yelling, resorting to personal criticisms or withdrawing from the discussion."

However, asking (and getting) our needs met is not just about speaking about them; it's about listening and the exchange we have through dialogue. When we listen deeply to the person we're communicating with, they feel heard and are more likely to be receptive and open to hearing us and/ or reciprocating. Relationships are all about giving and receiving, right?

In a romantic or intimate relationship, Barton Goldsmith also suggests that we:

- Discuss what specific behaviors you see that you don't feel good about.
- Make a single request at a time.
- State your request in gentle terms like, 'In the future would you be willing to...'.
- Tell your partner what you want, not what you don't want.
- Be honest, be clear and be kind.

Professionally

Margie Warrell offers more great advice that I find most useful applied to a professional situation, but that can also be used personally, if the context is right. People, especially women, do two things: 1) we play it safe and 2) we dilute a request to "minimize the possibility of being turned down" or to not be too much of a burden. In contrast to playing it safe, she recommends (and I agree) to "be bold and don't dilute" the request -- given the fact that people "rarely, if ever, are given more than what" we've asked for and because we "will nearly always end up with more than [we] would have received otherwise had [we] not been bold in [our] request."

To address the second point, she suggests thinking "about what [our] ideal outcome would be and then confidently, courageously, asking for it" -- not in an aggressive way, but "in a way that conveys that [we] know [our] worth."

Another way to get our needs met is to be clear in our communication. "It needs to specify not just 'what' [we'd] like but also the time frame in which [we] want it." For example, a professional request could be, "Will you provide input on the attached report by this Thursday at noon?" Want to be even more clear? If communicating by email, put your request in the header with what you need and by when and repeat that in the body of the message. One thing to be careful about here, however, is tone. You want to ask nicely and not be directive, especially with a peer or colleague in a higher position.

Yet in other types of professional settings, Alexandra Latos recommends that rather than say, "Will you please...?," say, "This needs to be done." Women often try to be too polite and accommodating, which may actually be telling others that we're "a doormat." What people need is "guidance on where they can and cannot step!"

In marketing, there is almost always a call-to-action at the end of a message, even if that action is as benign as "learn more". In sales and development, it's called the 'ask.' In correspondence with prospective customers, the sales person is supposed to have one 'ask' at each point during the prospect's life cycle – unless or until the prospect becomes a customer.

Consider this when you are also doing outreach or pitching an idea; answer the question, "what outcome do I want from this communication?" and then ask for it.

Photo by Mick Schultz, MixPix.

For instance, when "people seeking support for a cause, charity, or educational institution are trained in making the 'ask', they are told to not "pile on the reasons [for 'the ask']." Susan Krauss explains that "research by Dartmouth Psychologist, Daniel Feiler and colleagues showed that alumni were more likely to give money to their alma mater when given a single basis for the request." In this research, 'the ask' was either backed by an altruistic reason or egotistical reason – not both. "Find one reason to make your request, and give that the biggest play possible in order to ensure that you'll get a positive response in return." I will add that in order to select that one reason, you must think about who you are speaking to. In other words, know your audience. In this case, would that person be more motivated by altruism or their ego?'

In another for instance, I took a job that I originally didn't think I'd stay with because I was making a transition from freelancing to full-time work. The hiring manager who became my boss (a male) made an offer in writing with a particular salary. Months later, after I'd stopped looking for other work and lost my leverage, he reduced the offer by $5,000. At the time, I needed the job, so stuck with it under those conditions. Later, when I had reached my limit and was unwilling to accept this, I went to him and said, "I need [the originally agreed upon salary]." I believed I needed it, that I deserved it and was ready to walk away if he didn't provide it. The result? He raised my salary and added a base annual bonus to equal the original offer. It wasn't exactly what I'd asked for, but if I had not asked, I wouldn't have received anything.

Doing all of the above substantially increases the likeliness that our needs will be fulfilled and our self-confidence raised.

How to reinforce the behavior

Reward yourself or set up a reward system when you achieve results regardless of how large or small those results are. The reward can be big or small too. For instance, when I know I have chores to do around the house, I will push myself to do the chores first and then reward myself with a nice cup of tea afterwards or a lazy session on the couch in front of the TV. But the reward comes *after* the chore. If there's something at work I'm dreading to do or that's difficult, I will reward myself afterwards with a mindless task or something fun. It doesn't make doing the chores and tasks more fun, but it *does* help make me feel even better when I get the reward.

NEXT STEP –TIPS FOR GETTING YOUR NEEDS MET

Do's

1. Realize what some of your limiting thoughts are. Write them down.
2. Distinguish between your needs and others (refer to chapter on Boundaries).
3. Acknowledge which one(s) are ridiculous. Laugh about it and let it go.
4. Tell yourself you're worth it.

5. Replace those limiting thoughts with a list of needs, wants and/or goals, and again, write them down.
6. Identify next steps in achieving them and select the top three priorities at a time to help make those goals more accessible and easier to achieve.
7. Be honest about your request – both with yourself and the other person.
8. Consider the other person's situation when you are ready to "make the ask." If they are troubled or overwhelmed themselves, consider waiting until you notice they may be ready to give. Just don't make a pattern of waiting. In that case, your behavior is more due to avoiding the ask.
9. Ask for what you need with clear communication.
10. Be direct with a gentle, yet assertive delivery. Humor is also useful in getting a message across in a way that the person you're speaking to can receive it.
11. Celebrate success by rewarding yourself for a job well done!

Don'ts

1. Use "bait-and-switch" tactics by initially asking for something smaller and then incrementally making the request larger. This makes people feel resentful, and/or manipulated, reduces the likeliness you will get anything in the future and can damage the overall relationship.
2. Ask for too much or too little (in the case of negotiating).

3. Expect to be comfortable asking for things, especially if doing so is new to you.

4. Go back to the same people asking for things, unless there is a history of giving and receiving and/or you've recently given to them. This type of behavior creates what I call "solicitation fatigue" on the part of the receiver, which can 1) reduce the likeliness of you getting what you want, 2) put a strain on the relationship and/or 3) turn the person off completely.

Awake My Soul

And now my heart stumbles on things I don't know
My weakness I feel I must finally show
Lend me your hand and we'll conquer them all
But lend me your heart and I'll just let you fall
Lend me your eyes I can change what you see
But your soul you must keep, totally free
Har har, har har, har har, har har
Awake my soul, awake my soul
Awake my soul

-Mumford & Sons

#youwillalwaysgetmoreifyouask

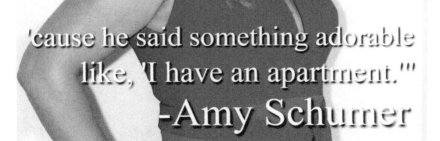

"I went home with this French guy

'cause he said something adorable like, 'I have an apartment.'"

-Amy Schumer

Chapter 10

On Dating: Where do I start?

Alas, we reach our final chapter - on dating. You will see that it's quite longer than the other chapters, perhaps because I've had so much experience on this topic.

In my 20's, I defined much of my worth and power through my sexuality. It was a way I could feel my power and obtain intimacy (when I wasn't taking on others' desires as my own). So, what did this look like? I dated men and slept with enough of them, giving something sacred away to some who were often undeserving. Don't get me wrong; sex is wonderful, but it needs to be respected. And unless you're able to completely disconnect emotionally (in cases where you need to just satisfy a temporary need and can maintain distance), I've come to believe that love needs to be there, as well as the respect. For women in particular, having multiple partners that you don't know well can be emotionally and energetically dangerous.

Photo by Mick Schultz, MixPix.

When I first worked on this chapter, I'd been dating for literally 30 years! It chokes me up and reminds of the scene in *Sex and the City* when Charlotte says, "I've been dating since I was 15! When is this going to happen? I'm tired!" *I feel you Charlotte, even though you're a fictional character.* I'm sure many other women relate; that's why *Sex and The City* was (and possibly still is) so popular. I've had four long-term relationships and one engagement. Still, no closed deal! I've been on five dating sites (yes, *five*). I've even experimented with taking time off from dating by instead going on meditation retreats, taking long spans of time just hanging out with girlfriends, etc., but haven't quite learned how to work with the universe in a way that appears to serve me.

My come to Jesus talk with my father and more

Shortly before my father passed away, I had what I'll call a "come to Jesus talk" with him about why he had cheated on my mother. He rationally and honestly responded and then added that 1) he'd be okay if I were with a woman and that 2) I'd scare off any man under 50. *I knew it!* I'd really opened things up with my direct question and my family thought I was gay! Finally, it's out! I'm not out, but their internal story was out...and "scare anyone under 50?" *C'mon!* I guess just as I was holding onto that question for years, he too had been holding onto those thoughts.

Around this time, I'd also read an article about a woman in her late 20's who was trying to get pregnant and was experimenting with fertility treatments. I remember thinking, *Really? You're stressed out in your late 20's... really?* This 20-something went on to say how she was born to bear children...that this was what her body was created for. *Eye roll.* It shocked me that women still believed their primary value comes from the ability to reproduce.

Bottom line though is that there's this underlying and overt pressure to be married and have children. So much so that, as a woman, you don't even know what you want vs. what other people want for you. *Totally anxiety provoking!* The pressure alone will push us into a space of unhealthy expectations about partnership and family. I consider myself to be a pretty authentic, in-touch-with-myself kind of person, so why was I affected by this? Perhaps it was the reason I could at least see how this messaging and pressure has the ability to create madness.

Don't give your power to others

Oh geez, I've done this one before. For me, it took the form of putting all of my trust in some men I'd date (as my therapist put it) and not having healthy boundaries. This manifested for me when I believed everything someone told me and completely followed their lead. An example of this was when I was with a boyfriend whom I loved very much (I mean deep, crazy in love-ness). The first time he broke up with me, he texted me 24 hours later saying he'd made a mistake and wanted me back. In the blink of an eye (or at least less than another 24 hours later), I welcomed him back into the relationship.

Months later, we got into an argument, and he said he needed to separate again from the relationship. Hurt again, but this time pissed off, I let him go and gave him his space. I did not email, text or call him. In fact, I didn't even post on social media, so there was absolutely no communication. After a month of being separated, he reached back out to me via a text *again* and said he wanted to meet and talk. We met to talk, and I thought it was the end, but he told me he wanted to try again... *again!* Shocked that he wanted to be back in the relationship, I invited him to stay with me that night, and we picked up where we left off. But by this time, I felt degraded throughout the remainder of the relationship, which lasted another several months. After a full year of seeing each other, we got into another fight, and he said he just couldn't handle it. Even a few months after the final break up, I'd hoped that he would come back, as he had done before, but I finally understood that I was worth more and cut ties with him completely. In the end, it came down to self-worth, and I had to take my power back.

In another example (there are so many!), I met a guy online. He lived in Bethesda, MD and I lived in Baltimore, MD – they're about 45 minutes apart. He came to see me for a first date, and it was a really fun, very innocent day activity; we went to a park for a picnic. He wanted to see me a second time and offered to come out to Baltimore again. For this date, we went to dinner near my house (you can see where this is going). We had a nice time at dinner, but he had had too many drinks to drive home, so asked if he could stay the night at my place and promised to "be good". I'd communicated my boundaries about sex and dating, and didn't want this near stranger in my home. I said no... *initially*. He kept pushing, and I started feeling badly, like if he drove home drunk and hurt someone or was hurt himself, I would somehow be responsible. And after all, he *had* come all this way to see me. I kind of owed him, right?

Well, he ended up spending the night and behaved himself during the official sleeping hours, but first thing in the morning (you know how men are), it was a nightmare. Dry humping, followed by penis out, followed by the beginnings of masturbation. You get the point. I still did not have sex with him (or anything else), but was so miserable and felt like I was beating him off with a stick (no pun intended – really!). He left my house apologizing, saying that he was just excited. We never spoke again, but I'm still haunted by that experience.

Be careful about who you allow in your space... particularly your intimate space

It recently dawned on me that women (and men) are programmed to believe that women are property to own, like a car, house or TV. I truly believe men think they have the right to a woman's body and that women, at least on some level, believe the same thing due to social programming... until we wake up. And sometimes this takes many years. This mindset becomes problematic and manifests in many ways. Of course, there is rape, which is the worst manifestation, but there is also what I'll call somewhat indiscriminate sex. Most of us have seen *Girls Gone Wild,* where a parent's nightmare is filmed on television: half-naked, young women drunk beyond consciousness putting themselves in precarious situations with men. I know this very well because I was one of them!

As an HSP

As an HSP, it may be even *more* challenging to 1) not get caught up in trying to match someone else's desire for us, 2) not try to want to please the person at any cost, 3) not over identify our value with theirs and 4) not be deeply affected by the ups and downs of the relationship(s). We have to be even *more* centered, more careful and have more space to know what we are truly feeling and where the boundaries between "us and them" start and end.

Photo by Mick Schultz, MixPix.

With all of these variables combined, you can imagine a very difficult situation, more so for women. I know we often feel pressure to be in partnership and have learned to measure our value by the man we end up with; we have been programmed to take responsibility for others problems (i.e. attract wounded puppies, so we can heal them). In the end, we have a number of hurdles to overcome. *So frustrating!*

THE SCIENCE BEHIND IT

This is what science has to say about it. Ellen Walker Ph.D., Clinical Psychologist and Author of "Complete Without Kids," describes in her article[36] the number of pressures women receive about relationships, families and having children. Among them are family, friends and the media, in other words, all the people women are surrounded by.

---

36 Dr. Walker, E. (2011, April). Direct and Subtle Pressure to Have Children—How Can a Childfree Wannabe Cope? *Psychology Today.*

You remember the song small children would sing to tease each other, "[so-AND-so] sitting-in-a tree, k-i-s-s-i-n-g. First comes love, then comes marriage, then comes a baby in the baby carriage." I remember singing this myself - often! *For all you millennials and younger people, you're welcome for the introduction to this song.*

More about the media

In her report, *Gendered Media: The Influence of Media on Views of Gender,* Scholar and Author, Julia T. Wood, focuses on the media and how it influences gender perception and roles in our society. We are talking movies, television *and* advertising! In addition to women being underrepresented, she finds that "men and women are portrayed in stereotypical ways", and that depictions of relationships between men and women emphasize traditional roles and normalize violence against women." According to her (and I agree), the media is full of "depictions of women as sex objects who are usually young, thin, beautiful, passive, dependent and often incompetent and dumb. Female characters (also) devote their primary energies to improving their appearances and taking care of homes and people."

This dynamic is effectively illustrated in the common types of advertising we are exposed to on a daily basis and shown in the sample advertising below. You see men in suits on the left side, looking very distinguished and perhaps off to their lucrative jobs. On the right, you see women barely covered in lingerie who appear they are ready for sex.

"The irony of this representation is that the very qualities women are encouraged to develop (beauty, sexiness, passivity, and powerlessness) in order to meet cultural ideals of femininity contribute to their victimization. Also, the qualities that men are urged to exemplify (aggressiveness, dominance, sexuality, and strength) are identical to those linked to abuse of women."

Who dominates the media? White men! *Let me put my surprise face on.* According to an article in *USA Today*[37], "in 2017...(Directors Guild of America) found that among those films to make at least $250,000 at the box office, 12 percent of directors were women and 10 percent were people of color."

According to a *Time* article and report from the University of Southern California, the numbers are even lower. In the report[38], "1,100 of top grossing movies released between 2007 and 2017 found that only 4% of those films' directors were women." And confirms that "film directors are still overwhelmingly white and male."

But that's not all! It's in our biology!
Biologically, women release the same hormone during sex that they do when they breastfeed their children, so it's much easier to get attached. I'm referring to the hormone oxytocin.

---

37 Study: Hollywood directors still mostly white and male, study finds by Associate Press, *USA Today*. June 21, 2018.
38 Cooney, S. (2018, January). The Number of Women Who Direct Hollywood Movies Is Still Embarrassingly Small. *Time.*

In her article, "Oxytocin: The Love and Trust Hormone Can Be Deceptive[39]," Rita Watson, MPH, has something to say about it. "Often called the love drug, oxytocin plays a role in bonding, maternal instinct, enduring friendship, marriage, and orgasms."...."Oxytocin increases...positive evaluation of others."

"After making love, a woman might mistake the oxytocin release for feelings that tell her, 'This is your perfect partner.'" As Professor Emerita at California State University, Dr. Breuning notes, "Despite those initial feelings, it does not necessarily mean that the person is trustworthy." *Duh. As most women can attest to.* And immediately after the encounter, many will obsess about the encounter itself. Ladies, you know what I'm talking about. Breuning attributes this to a "perception you have

39 Watson, R. MPH. (2013, October). Oxytocin: The Love and Trust Hormone Can Be Deceptive. *Psychology Today.*

at the moment [that] is an illusion you create about the person that may or may not fit what happens next."

Health and medical Journalist, Anna Hodgekiss, also makes a clear distinction between what happens to women vs. men during and after sex, based on hormones. In her article, "Sex: Why it makes women fall in love but just makes men want MORE!"[40], she indicates that "a key hormone released during sex (for women) is oxytocin, also known as the 'cuddle hormone'...is also the key to bonding, as it increases levels of empathy. Women produce more of this hormone...and this means they are more likely to let their guard down and fall in love with a man after sex."

"The problem is that when a man has an orgasm, the main hormone released is dopamine — the pleasure hormone," which rather than forming an attachment, merely leaves him wanting more – and not necessarily from the same woman!

Bottom line? Don't be fooled by your hormones! Because human beings are connected energetically, that random person's energy is now in your intimate space. You need to give yourself a little time to know whether it's safe to let your guard down and know (at least somewhat) who you're inviting into that space.

---

40 Hodgekiss, A. (2011, August). Sex: Why it makes women fall in love - but just makes men want MORE! *Daily Mail.*

NEXT STEP - DOS AND DON'TS

Do

1. Trust your feelings. "If it feels bad," as my Therapist sister says, "it usually *is* bad."
2. Wait to reveal yourself until you feel safe with a person, and after they have shown you that they care and respect you.
3. Try your hardest to wait to have sex with the person until you believe that both you and s/he want to be in a relationship with each other and after a conversation has taken place about this -- unless you and your partner are clear that you 1) just want to have fun and/or 2) agree to an open relationship.
4. In a highly emotionally charged situation, don't make sudden decisions. Give yourself time to respond. At the very least, wait 24-48 hours to think about things.
5. Use protection! Use protection! Use protection!
6. If you meet someone online and agree to meet in person, send pictures and the high-level descriptors you know about him/her to a friend or relative (e.g. his/her name, age, occupation, where you're meeting and when, place of work, where s/he lives, etc.).
7. If you meet someone online, meet him/her in a neighborhood you're comfortable with and in public. Also make sure you have cash on you and a way to get home easily.

Don't

1. Agree to something that makes you uncomfortable. You will end up resentful or hurt in the end.
2. Remain in a degrading situation, even if you're afraid of the alternative and/or you love the person.
3. Invite someone you met online into your home in fewer than three dates unless you expect and want to have sex with him/her. (**Note**: This is still a risk to your safety as s/he is a complete stranger).
4. Have more than two drinks on a first date with someone you met online. This probably applies to any way you're introduced to someone, but you are more likely to attract the dodgy element via the internet.
5. Have someone you meet online pick you up or drop you off on the first date.

In Closing

There you have it! 100+ pages of life by Heather Gwaltney. We've covered a lot, addressing topics from sensitivity to meditation to science to dating. I think that's called comprehensive. Hopefully by now, you are feeling at least a little more validated, positive, and (dare I say) inspired. I've put considerable love into each chapter and hope that the love has come through. Are you feeling it?

Final thoughts I'd like to leave with you

1. Read parts of the book over again any time you need a reminder...or would like to have a good laugh at my expense.

2. We all have sacred light inside of us and the power to do amazing work in the world! Do not let anyone tell you otherwise.
3. Stand by other women. Unity prevails!

At last

...The skies above are blue
My heart was wrapped up in clover
The night I looked at you
I found a dream that I could speak to
A dream that I can call my own
I found a thrill to press my cheek to
A thrill that I have never known
Oh yeah yeah
You smiled, you smiled
Oh and then the spell was cast
And here we are in heaven
For you are mine...
At Last

-Etta James

#takethegoodandleavetherest

Shout Out

In an effort to raise funds and complete this book, we ran a crowdfunding campaign. I want to give a "shout out" to all of the donors who gave and give special attention to our larger contributors, Erin Essenmacher, Gerry Quintanilla Alex Cook and Naomi Helene!

To loved ones who listened to me compulsively talk about this book, big hugs and kisses to you.

Please accept my deepest gratitude. Your generosity is greatly appreciated!

About The Author

Heather Gwaltney describes herself as an artist, writer, business woman, egalitarian, environmentalist, meditator and Reiki Master. As the book reflects, her experiences have brought her into numerous environments, including the typical 9-5 workplace, the art world and the spiritual community.

Heather's "left-brained" professional experience is primarily in marketing, communications and organizational development, where she has worked for over 20 years in the private, non-profit and education sectors. Heather has also taught courses at George Mason University and delivered in-person and online trainings for a number of nonprofits and private companies. Now, she manages programs and creates communications for print, web, video and social media.

She holds a Masters in Organizational Development and a Bachelors in Psychology with a Business Minor. As a 20-year veteran of meditation and energy work, her certifications include Mindfulness Meditation, Reiki: Master Level and Permaculture Design. She is currently enrolled in a Mindfulness Meditation Teacher program and will obtain certification in 2021, at which point, she will be able to better help companies and individuals apply the practice to everyday life with compassion and humor.

Heather's biggest advocacy passions are the environment and gender equity. Her greatest love (outside of loved ones) is meditation, and her greatest artistic achievements have been a documentary called *Ageless* and this book for women. She currently resides in a neighborhood outside of Washington, DC.

Connect with Heather and learn more about her work by visiting her documentary website at https://heathergwaltney.com.